# LET'S GET GOING!

---

# LET'S GET GOING!

From oral history interviews with
Arthur M. Smith, Jr., a narrative
interpretation by R. T. King.

Publication of *Let's Get Going!* was made possible in part
by a grant from the First Interstate Bank of Nevada Foundation

*Library of Congress Cataloging-in-Publication Data:*

Smith, Arthur M., 1922-
    Let's get going : from oral history interviews with Arthur M.
Smith, Jr. : a narrative interpretation / by R.T. King.
        p.  cm.
    Includes index.
    ISBN 1-56475-371-9 (cloth)
    1. Smith, Arthur M., 1922-  . 2. Bankers—Nevada—Biography.
3. First Interstate Bank of Nevada—History. 4. Banks and banking
—Nevada—History. I. King, R. T. (Robert Thomas), 1944-
II. Title.
HG2463.S55A3    1996
332.1'092—dc20
[B]                                                    96-43603
                                                        CIP

*Publication Staff:*
*Production Manager:* Linda J. Sommer
*Senior Production Assistant:* Terri Genovese
*Production Assistants:* Verne W. Foster,
Amy Frank, Nancy Vu

# Contents

# Preface

WHEN THE INFANT Arthur M. Smith, Jr. arrived in Nevada
with his parents in 1922, about 75,000 people lived in
the state. Eighty percent of Nevada's population was
rural. Mining, ranching, and railroading were the
foundations of its economy, and casino gaming was
forbidden by law. Nevada's population grew by about 40
percent before Art graduated from high school, but that
growth was largely associated with the construction of
Hoover Dam and the location of war industries and
military facilities in Clark County—the economic and
social profiles of the rest of the state were hardly
affected. Few could have foreseen the astonishing
changes which were soon to occur in Nevada and in the
lives of many of her citizens.

After a year at the University of Nevada and a brief
stint as a hostler's helper with the Southern Pacific
Railroad, Art Smith spent eighteen months as a clerk in
the Sparks branch of the First National Bank before

leaving home in 1943, bound for naval pilot training. No matter what happened, he was certain that he was through with banking forever. He was wrong. Immediately after the war jobs were scarce; Art's resolve weakened, and he took work with the Bank of Nevada in Las Vegas just until a commercial pilot's seat opened up. It was a good decision. Art never did become an airline pilot, but thirty-eight years later he retired as chairman of the board and chief executive officer of First Interstate Bank of Nevada, which, with sixty-five branches, was by far the largest bank in the state.

Art Smith was an extremely accomplished and successful banker. He was also lucky. With the end of World War II, Nevada commenced a truly remarkable economic and demographic metamorphosis, and Art was there—the right man with the right abilities in the right place at the right time. He plunged in, and his career swept ahead on a wave of unprecedented population growth and economic expansion. By the time Art retired from banking in 1984, Nevada's population was eight times greater than it had been when he started. That explosive growth (and the success of the businesses that sustained it and profited from it) was propelled almost entirely by casino gaming—the industry's revenues had expanded by a phenomenal 14,000 percent, from $21.5 million in 1946 to $3 billion a year by 1984. In the span of Art Smith's career Nevada had been transformed from a raw frontier state with a small, widely scattered population into a booming, urban, air-conditioned tourist destination. Mining, agriculture and railroads hardly mattered anymore, but banking was in the middle of everything.

*Let's Get Going!* is both Art Smith's story and the story of an extraordinary period in Nevada history as seen from the perspective of a railroad machinist's son who became a top banker. During thirty hours of tape recorded interviewing, Art and I covered a wide range of subjects. From life in Sparks in the 1930s, to running a state bank in Las Vegas in the booming, wide open 'fifties and 'sixties, to sixteen years in Reno as the head of the most powerful bank in Nevada, Art's story is filled with illuminating firsthand information about many of the events, people, and phenomena that shaped the Nevada of today.

Art's excellent powers of recall, his quick wit, and his congenial personality made him a pleasure to interview; but the verbatim transcript from which *Let's Get Going!* was composed totals over one thousand pages and is difficult to read and understand in its raw form. Oral discourse can be practically impenetrable when represented in print: empty of gesture, inflection, tone, and other nuances that go unrecorded on tape, or for which there are no symbols on the keyboard, transcripts are full of fractured syntax, false starts, repetition, and general disorder. Researchers willing to accept the challenge of reading oral history transcripts often find them to be important sources of information, but the form will never reach a wide audience.

In order to make the content of Art Smith's oral history more accessible to the average reader, I have composed a narrative interpretation in his voice. Its oral origins notwithstanding, in general the text reads like that of any other book, but the reader will encounter two unconventional devices that are employed to represent the dynamic of spoken language: [laughter] appears when Art laughs in amusement or to express irony; and ellipses are used not to indicate that material has been deleted, but that a statement is being made haltingly . . . or there is a pause for dramatic effect. In addition, the natural episodic structure of oral history leads to an occasional lack of smooth transition from subject to subject, and when this occurs it is indicated in the text by a break between paragraphs.

Art Smith has read the finished manuscript of his story in page proof form and affirmed in writing that it accurately interprets the content of the interviews from which it is drawn. However, as with all oral histories, while the University of Nevada Oral History Program (UNOHP) can vouch for the authenticity of *Let's Get Going!*, it does not claim that the recollections upon which the book is based are entirely free of error. It should be approached with the same caution that a prudent reader exercises when consulting government records, newspaper accounts, diaries, and other sources of historical information.

Publication of *Let's Get Going!* would not have been possible without external funding. It has reached print in large part because Larry Tuntland and Mendy

Cavanagh believed in the value of our project and were instrumental in securing the generous support of the First Interstate Bank of Nevada Foundation. We are grateful to Mr. Tuntland, Ms. Cavanagh, and the Foundation.

R. T. KING
University of Nevada, Reno

# Part One

*Finding My Way*

ALMOST EVERY SUMMER DAY when I was a kid I'd go over to the railroad shops to see my dad and hang around with him while he was working on engines. I was really a railroading nut—I practically lived in the switching yards watching trains come and go; and since some of my friends' fathers were conductors or engineers, my pals and I were often up in a caboose going to Imlay, or on a high-speed passenger train headed for Carlin, riding in the cab of the engine. It was a way of life for us—we were *certain* that we would grow up and go to work for the railroad. Many of my old pals did just that. They went to work for the railroad; they married their high school sweethearts; they stayed home. I took a different path . . . .

# 1

## *Mom Ran The Joint*

MY MOTHER AND FATHER[1] must have met through some Mormon activity, because in those days that's about all there was to do in Utah. The Mormon Church had something going almost every night if you had the time or the interest. When they started seeing each other Dad was living in Providence and Mom was living in Brigham City—quite a distance for Dad to travel. After they married, Dad worked on a farm outside of Logan; and then following my birth (May 2, 1922) he learned that there were openings in the railroad shops in Sparks, Nevada. So he traveled to Sparks, got a job and a place to stay, and sent for my mom and me. We took a train and arrived in Sparks when I was six weeks old.

In their Sparks yards the Southern Pacific Railroad had a big repair facility, what they called the back shop.

---

[1]  Elva Evelyn Knudson and Arthur M. Smith

They'd move huge cabin-front engines, biggest loco-motives in the world, into the shop, and tear them down and lay every part out on the floor, replace or repair it, then put the engines back together. The engines would come out like new. Dad hired on there as a machinist's helper, and after a lengthy apprenticeship he became a machinist in the back shop.

Over the years Dad kept getting promotions. Even-tually he became a federal inspector whose job was to check certain parts of locomotives—see that there was enough lubrication, and that this worked and that worked. One day an engine that he'd inspected left Sparks at the head of an eastbound train which changed crews at Imlay, and then Carlin, and then Montello. It was rushing across the Great Salt Lake trestle, 500 miles east of Sparks, when a backfire blew out the firebox door, burning the fireman's hands. For this, my father lost his job. In those days they fired you, and *then* they launched an investigation. [laughter]

Within twenty-four hours after Dad was fired, the relief society, which was the wives of the guys at the Mormon Church, had our house so full of canned vegetables and milk and clothes and stuff that we could hardly move around. Mormons stick together and care for one another, but our family was no different from many others going through hard times during the Depression: You'd go to the bank and say you couldn't pay the mortgage on time, but you'd get it to them soon; instead of two quarts of milk a day, you'd have one delivered; and we always had a garden in the back yard, so vegetables on the table was just automatic—every Saturday morning before I could play, I had to go weed that damned garden! [laughter]

To help make ends meet Dad got on with the WPA, taking a shovel in his hand and going to work on a road project. He didn't have to do that for long. Soon the railroad had a big investigation into the incident, and all the engineers and firemen got up and said, "Hey, wait! There's no reason to fire this guy. *None* of the firebox door latches work properly. Every engine that goes out of here has them that way. We drive trains all day long, and we've had firebox doors in much worse shape than that." Dad got his job back.

Most marriages don't work as designed (the British royal families have proved that), but my parents' marriage worked almost as if it had been planned. You can't have two leaders in a marriage; you can't have two followers; and in our family my mother was the leader and Dad basically was the follower. He was a great provider and a wonderful father, but Mom ran the joint, and she handled the household finances entirely. She decided when it was time to buy a car; she decided when it was time to paint the house. Whatever was going to happen, Mom was the one who said, "Now is the time!" That included disciplining us kids. I don't think my father ever laid a hand on me, even when he should have whacked me, but Mom had no qualms about sending me over to the ditch to cut a willow so she could beat on me with it. [laughter] Or she would withhold something that I wanted, "until you learn to behave." Mom was perpetual motion: if she was making a cake, she never stopped; if she was cleaning house, she never stopped; and if she was giving me hell, she never stopped.

For several years after we moved to Sparks my folks rented from the Tholl family, and we lived about three doors down from their place. When I was very young I'd walk over to their house in my flannel pajamas to see my pal, Bud Tholl. His mom would put out two big bowls of oatmeal, and we'd sit there and eat it, me in my pajamas. We rented from the Tholls for years, but Mom wouldn't accept renting as anything but a temporary measure. She was going to have her own house, and she worked hard and saved every penny so that we could buy one. (To help support the family Mom worked at J. C. Penney's as a sales clerk in dry goods and later in women's clothing.)

Mom and Dad bought our first house from an old guy named Gunther, and the mortgage was twenty-five dollars a month. That house was on Fourteenth Street, across from the junior high school. I was never late to school until I lived across the street from it: I'd wait to hear the bells ring before leaving for class. Later they sold that house and bought two houses on a lot—we lived in one and rented one. Then they bought a larger house at the corner of Seventeenth (now Rock) and B Streets, and that's where we lived while I was going to high school.

Our house on Fourteenth Street was right next to a power station. You could hear those transformers hum all day and night. We had two bedrooms, a living room, and a kitchen—it wasn't much, but for those days it was nice. I shared a bedroom with my brother Robert, who was three years younger than me. Underneath the house, my father built a basement—single-handedly dug it and wheel-barrelled the earth out. He put a furnace in the basement to heat the house, and he built a little play-room for us kids down there.

Our next-door neighbor, a guy named George Keele, was a school teacher. He and his wife had four boys and a daughter, Ora. She and I were kind of childhood sweethearts, and Mrs. Keele was almost like a second mother to me. If I was over at their place and did something wrong, Aunt Roxie (Mrs. Keele) didn't hesitate to belt me just like I was one of her own kids. [laughter]

Education was valued in our family. Dad had graduated from Utah State, and Mom had gone through high school. I started school at Robert H. Mitchell Elementary, and I enjoyed it. My pals and I had fun. You took your lunch, and you'd go outside and eat it on the playground. Mom would pack me a peanut butter and jelly sandwich or . . . we didn't get turkey and beef and those sorts of things like you do now. She'd also pack me a pint Mason jar filled with milk, and I'd sit and drink that with my sandwich and take the Mason jar home so Mom could refill it the next morning. Every boy carried a bag of marbles, and at recess and lunch break we'd run out and draw a big circle in the dirt and play marbles. Each guy had one or two fancy agates that he kept in his pocket. You didn't put them in the game, but you were always trying to get the other guy to put his in.

Math was always my favorite subject. I did well in it, and I really excelled at business math, which Mr. Keele taught in the ninth grade. Evelyn Mantle taught us English and civics and history. I felt like history was just something you had to get through—it's there and you can't avoid it. [laughter] If you misbehaved, Mrs. Mantle whacked you on the hand with a ruler, so when she told you to do something, you did it! And then if you were real bad, you went to the principal's office. He had a big paddle, and he whacked you right on the butt: "Get your act together and get back in there and do what she says!"

In the ninth grade I signed up for band. I played a little old beat-up cornet. Kenneth Ball, the music director, started me in the fourth chair, and I'd improve a little and move along a little, and finally, when I got really interested, my folks bought me a Conn trumpet. I practiced a lot. If I had nothing to do, I'd get my horn out and maybe just blow scales for practice; not regular music, but trying to improve my technique. I'd sit in the living room and just blow the horn. Finally, my mother would say, "Would you like to take that outside for a while?"

When I was thirteen my sister Margery was born, and soon after that the family bought property out on

Seventeenth street. The big white house had three bedrooms and a huge glassed-in front porch, which had another bedroom in it. That's where we were living when I graduated from high school. When my father worked the day shift, he went in at seven thirty and he was off at three thirty, and when my mom was working at J. C. Penney's, she started at ten o'clock and got off at six; so sometimes nobody was there when my brother and I came home from school. We had a key hidden underneath the house some place, but I don't remember ever locking the doors unless we were going out of town.

Dad had served in the Navy in the First World War—he was on the battleship *Minnesota* when she was torpedoed by a submarine about six hundred miles off Norfolk. She didn't sink, but Dad couldn't swim, and it was a frightening experience for him. My mother took great delight in telling a story about his inability to swim: While he was in the Navy he had a girl friend, and once when they were riding the roller coaster at the Norfolk Beach amusement park, their car jumped the track and plunged into the ocean. Dad's girl friend had to save him from drowning. He was a true swabby. [laughter]

If you hadn't served in the military, Dad felt you really hadn't got it all done yet; but once you'd served, you were something special. Veterans affairs was his biggest interest, and he eventually became commander of the American Legion post. He liked to be involved in things. He was in the Sparks Volunteer Fire Department, and when there was a fire the bell rang in our ears and woke us all up, and Dad would pull on his boots and away he'd go. Dad even served a term on the Sparks city council in the 1930s. (He and Mom were Republicans.) He didn't get re-elected, but I think it was just because someone got up and made more noise than he did. He was very gentle, and I don't think I ever saw him mad; Dad was always the guy who kept the machinery oiled.

Mom and Dad were devout Mormons, and Sparks was a big Mormon community. When I was young, the Mormon Church was about it, the center of everything. You didn't even realize there was another religion. While you're still very young you begin going to Primary on Monday afternoons. When you get older you get into Mutual, and eventually you start going to the meetings on Sunday. You don't have any choice, you just go. When you go to Sunday school, you go through four different classes. Then in the afternoon, you go to church. I don't know how many hours were taken up by all this, but whatever was available, you went to it. It was just a fact of life. But I didn't get any religious instruction at home, and I never read the *Book of Mormon*. (They don't make you read it.)

While I was going to Mutual, the church was the focus of my social life. When I got older and didn't have to go, it disappeared from my life entirely. In truth, I don't actually know much about the religion. The thing I remember most is something they called the Words of Wisdom: Don't smoke; don't drink; don't overindulge . . .

a list of common sense things that they hammered on constantly. But I went right out and smoked anyway. [laughter]

I was in the Boy Scouts. That didn't last long . . . it was a disaster. My troop met in the basement of the Robert H. Mitchell School, in the furnace room. Oliver Hansen, our Scout Master, was a wonderful fellow, but some of us had a little trouble accepting his regimentation. One night after a meeting we expressed our feelings: we raised the hood of his car and urinated all over the engine. When he started it up, the aroma wasn't too pleasing. Hansen learned who had done it. He held a formal court martial, ripped our badges off our uniforms and said, "You're out!" [laughter] And we were. (Much later in life, while I was a banker in southern Nevada, I got back in. Briefly in the 1950s I was vice president of the Boulder Dam Area Council of Boy Scouts, and then, after my bank transferred me to Reno, I was president of the Reno council for two years. I got the Silver Beaver Award for my service to the Scouts.)

I was much more interested in aviation than in Scouting. I would ride my bicycle out to the airport at the end of Gentry Lane and sit and watch the airplanes come and go. In those days it was a big deal. A United flight came every night about eight, and even if you hadn't had your supper yet, you'd still ride out there to see it land. Boeing 247-D's—they taxied right into the hangar where they'd unload and get serviced; then they'd load up, taxi out, and away they'd go again.

In the summer Mom and Dad would always rent a little cabin up at Carnelian Bay on Lake Tahoe for a week. Mom would go up first with us kids, and we'd get settled in. Dad was working the swing shift those days, and he'd come up after work. We'd swim in the lake and eat and wander around. It was a big deal.

Dad could get railroad passes for all of us, so once in a while we'd go over to San Francisco to knock around, and they'd show us the cable cars. There were no bridges across the bays back then. At the Carquinez Straits they took the train apart and put it on a barge and towed it across and put it back together; then it went on down to the Oakland mole, which was the end of the line. You boarded a ferry there to cross to San Francisco. I was probably about eight or nine years old the first time we did this, and we crossed the bay on the old *Berkeley* and stayed at the Powell Hotel.

# 2

*Life at The Farm*

OF ALL MY GRANDPARENTS I knew Grandmother Knudson best, because she lived the longest. She was still alive while I was in elementary school, and every year my mother would take us kids to Brigham City to visit two or three weeks with her. Then Dad would come in and spend a couple of days, and we'd go up where his family was. My Smith grandparents had named their farm Edgewood Hall. It sat up on what was called a "bench," kind of a plateau overlooking the little village of Providence, just southeast of Logan, Utah. The place seemed huge to me. The two-story house had six or seven bedrooms and a big back porch, and it was surrounded by tree nurseries. Grandfather Smith, who had died before I was born, had run cattle up in the foothills behind the house—they must've had four or five hundred acres up there.

Grandfather Smith had been born in England, and Grandmother Smith in Wales. They were from families that converted to Mormonism before emigrating to Utah. Grandmother's family was among the earliest settlers of the town of Providence, and she and Grandpa met there and were married in 1878. Grandpa was an educated man, had a big library, and he became a successful farmer and businessman—a prominent citizen in northern Utah. Once he was even offered an ambassadorship to Switzerland, which he turned down. His holdings were extensive. At one time he must have owned half of Idaho Falls, but he lost that property in the depression of 1897.

Grandpa Knudson had been born in Copenhagen, and Grandma Knudson was from Stockholm. They had homesteaded outside Brigham City, Utah. Today Pioneer Park encloses their old log cabin, and a plaque tells you how they raised their family there. Grandpa Knudson had run sheep and cattle, and owned lots of land. When the panic of 1897 hit, a big shipment of his cattle was in an Omaha stockyard waiting to be sold. He decided to keep them there and feed them until the price of beef came back; but the price never came back, and he lost a good deal of his fortune. Besides being a farmer and a rancher, he had hunted ducks for market in the Bear River Marsh. A photo shows one of his skiffs with maybe twenty shotguns mounted on it, all aimed forward—he'd quietly poke that thing out of the reeds near a flock of ducks, and pull the trigger string and shoot all the guns off at once; kill the ducks while they were still on the water. Then he'd bring them home, and pick them and clean them and ship them to New York

14

restaurants for a nickel a duck. I just marveled at the thought of that! Grandpa owned a big part of the marsh, and he sold it to a bunch of guys from New York who loved to shoot ducks. They were millionaires, so they named it the Millionaire Duck Club; later it became the Bear River Duck Club.

All those acres of land that my grandparents had owned were gone by the time I came along, but there was still the ten acre Knudson farm on the outskirts of Brigham City, and I would visit my Grandma there. Her old brick house was huge, with an enormous living room, dining room, kitchen, and basement. The front door never opened—you entered through the back door into the kitchen, a typical oldtime kitchen where everyone always congregated. Upstairs were four bedrooms, and the dining room and living room were downstairs. Nobody ever went into the living room . . . I think I may have walked through it once. [laughter]

There was no running water in Grandma's house, and no toilet facilities. Outside was a deep well, capped with a pump where you drew your water. Once a week, Saturdays, we bathed in big old tubs—there were three or four of them, and all of us kids would go out back and sit and splash. About fifty yards away was the outhouse, which Grandma had put at the end of a wide pathway, with lilacs on both sides and all around it.

I may have been Grandma Knudson's favorite. Anytime I went to visit her, she had all the things I liked (I loved peanut butter, and she always had peanut butter for me), and when she went out to pick raspberries or strawberries, she would say, "Arthur has to go with me; I want Arthur to help me pick the berries." Grandmother Knudson was just . . . she was Grandma!

When Grandma died, her only son, Edgar, kept the Knudson place, got it from the rest of her kids, and after I was eight years old I spent part of each summer there with him. Life at the farm was just . . . I could hardly wait to get on a train and go to Brigham City to Uncle Edgar's house! He had a horse that he harnessed for plowing and cultivating, and he grew cantaloupe, eggplant, tomatoes, two kinds of cherries, peaches and apricots on his ten acres. From the farm, I could walk to Brigham City's main street in fifteen minutes. The railroad went right through town, and I'd sit there by the hour watching steam trains go through.

The first time I traveled alone to see Uncle Edgar, my father got me a railroad pass. I was eight years old. Mom took me to the train, put me in my pajamas (it was about eight at night), tucked me in an upper berth, and pinned a note on me that said, "His Uncle Edgar will be waiting for him at Ogden." She gave the porter a dollar to watch over me. The train took off, and I went to sleep, and the porter woke me up and said, "It's time to get up and get dressed." When I got up, we were in Ogden, and there was Uncle Edgar waiting for me.

Uncle Edgar was a wonderful guy, and I had some second cousins that lived across the railroad tracks from him. We were inseparable; we just went everywhere together. I'd come home at night, and Uncle Edgar would be finished with his farm work, and he'd cook dinner and we'd go to bed. Even sleep together. It was always a sad day when I had to get on the train to go back to Sparks, because I loved my Uncle Edgar so much. All the fun I had . . . I didn't have a care in the world when I went to Brigham City in the summer. In fact, when my mother would get there for her two weeks it kind of slowed me down, because she started making me do things.

When I was twelve Uncle Edgar said, "I'll teach you how to shoot ducks." In those days the greatest duck shooting in the world was in the Bear River Delta just outside of Brigham City. I mean, you couldn't see the sun for the ducks! I had an old Remington automatic, and I packed that baby, and Uncle Edgar'd take me out. We had so much fun. In those days you could shoot twenty ducks, and I'd go out and shoot twenty in the morning, then take them down to the cherry orchard on his farm and pick them, then go back in the afternoon and shoot another twenty!

Mr. Leland Larson probably had as much influence on my life as anyone. He lived next door to the Knudson farm, and I used to play with his daughters when I was young. Later, when I was old enough to go around with him and help him with projects, he and I became almost inseparable.

Mr. Larson was just a nice, easy-going guy. If you didn't know him well you'd never guess what a keen mind he had. He loved to experiment with hybridizing trees and plants, and he kept crossing different varieties

17

of strawberries until he came up with a great break-through. How many times have you bitten into a strawberry that looks red and ripe on the outside, only to discover that it's whitish and hard on the inside? All strawberries used to ripen that way, from the outside in. Leland Larson developed one that ripened from the inside out, and he named it the Lindalicious, after Linda, the youngest of his three daughters. He made a lot of money on that.

He was also a bee keeper. The Superior Honey Company down in Ogden, Utah, would send up a whole box car just for his honey. I couldn't believe that there was that much honey in the world! When the honey came off, I'd go out and work with him with his bees, and he taught me an awful lot about them. He had no son, and when I hit there in the summer I just became his son—everything he did, I was with him. When we went out to tend the bees, I was with him, and when we took the honey off and extracted it, I was with him.

One day Mr. Larson told me that a swarm of bees had gotten in a cave by Promontory Point. They'd swarmed many times there, and he thought the big cave would be plumb full of honey. "You and I are going to go out there and look around," he said. Well, when we got out there we found so many bees that you couldn't tell whether it was insects or smoke drifting in and out of this cave . . . literally millions of bees. We had smokers and netted hats and everything, and we put on all the protective clothing we could find, because we knew we were going to make them mad. We put a great big tarpaulin and two brand new scoop shovels in his three-quarter ton pickup truck, and we drove up there and started loading honey comb—just scooped it out and threw it on the tarp in the truck. Honey's heavy; you couldn't take a full shovel scoop. We did that all morning, then we went back to his place and ran the honey through his extractors. I don't know how many tons we took out of that cave. It was just a real mess, but it was a great experience.

Leland Larson taught me more about how to live than anyone I was ever around. Here's this one guy, he was just . . . his life wasn't driven by an agenda as far as I could see: "Whatever you have to do, get it done today; and then tomorrow we'll do what comes along." If he had disappointments, I didn't see any. Maybe it was just that I was at the age where I needed someone to say, "Come on, we'll go tend the bees." I thought so much of Lee that later in life, when I received the DeMolay Legion of Honor, I invited him and his wife to come to Las Vegas to stay with Charlotte and me the night I got the award. He was like a second father to me.

# 3

## *Never Be Poor*

MY PARENTS WERE GOOD PEOPLE, but they had very little money. Anxiety about making ends meet sometimes made my mom cry, and when I was still a young boy I vowed that I would never be poor.

I began riding on a White Clover Dairy delivery truck when I was twelve. Early in the morning before school the driver would swing by, and I'd ride with him as he made his rounds. He'd stop the truck in front of a house and say, "They get two quarts," and I'd run and put two bottles on the steps and bring the empties back. Then when I was fourteen I went out to the dairy and badgered its owner, Ralph Smith, to give me real work. He did. Along with some other kids, I was hired to bottle milk. The pay was fifty cents a day, plus room and board.

I would get out of school at three thirty, and run to the dairy and bottle milk until about five thirty. Then we'd go in and have dinner. I stayed at the dairy, but I was on the junior high basketball team, and on game nights I'd have to run in to town to play. Then I'd run back out to the dairy and go to bed. They'd get us up at four thirty in the morning, and we'd bottle the milk and then eat and get cleaned up and run all the way in to school.

My parents knew the people who owned the dairy, and they thought the arrangement was fine. It was good for me; I was learning how to work and save money, I wasn't getting in trouble, and my grades didn't suffer. It wasn't like I had said, "Hell, I'm leaving home!" Anyway, our house was across the street from school, so I always went home at noon to eat lunch, see the parents, and pick up clean clothes or anything else I needed.

In the summer, when I didn't have to go to school, I'd work a longer day at the dairy—bottle milk and wash the bottles and steam them, and run the creamer and make cream. For that, they paid me a dollar a day. When you work for a dollar a day it doesn't add up very quickly, you know—you're always buying a pair of overalls or something—but when I needed five bucks, I had five bucks. Soon I was able to buy a bicycle, and my buddies thought I must be a millionaire: "Jesus, Smith, where'd you get the money?" But they weren't working every day.

I was with the dairy for four years, counting the time I rode with the delivery man, and I put money in the bank. But when I really got involved in high school activities, I couldn't handle the schedule anymore. I had to quit. Then I took up a paper route. You can't believe the paper route I had!

Reno had two newspapers—the *Nevada State Journal* came out in the morning, and the *Reno Evening Gazette* in the afternoon. N. B. Epperson was the *Gazette* distributor in Sparks: he had the contract; he had the franchise; and he was buying the papers. Every paper that was sold in Sparks, whether it was at a newsstand or delivered, he got a piece of it. Bud Tholl and I worked for Epperson. He provided us with an old Star Whippet—he paid for the whole thing, gas and car. Quite an arrangement.

We'd drive up to the *Gazette*'s plant, go downstairs and get about fourteen hundred papers. After rolling two hundred of them we'd start toward Sparks down Fourth Street, which was Highway 40 in those days. About where the old Threlkel ball park was, just as we were leaving Reno, we'd start throwing papers out the window into people's yards and against storefronts. We were heavy on the throttle, and we'd be speeding along, throwing those newspapers. [laughter] We'd go in there behind the Coney Island Bar and back and forth down through those neighborhoods and deliver about a hundred papers that way . . . end up down at Kellison & Poncia's, which was a newsstand up front with a saloon behind it. There was a shed out back, and eight or ten boys would be waiting for us there. I'd give them about twelve hundred papers, and they'd roll them, load them on their bikes, and ride off to their delivery routes.

We'd deliver the remaining papers from our car, starting down through what was called "the reserve," where John Ascuaga's is now. From Pyramid Way down to Fifteenth Street, it was all houses in there. Then up to the mental hospital. I'd drop twenty papers off with one of the patients who wasn't violent, and he'd deliver them to the others. Then down what is Glendale Road now, tossing papers on farm house lawns and sticking them in mail boxes . . . . We'd end up clear over on Sullivan Lane.

In those days I think a paper cost seventy-five cents a month, delivered. I'd get ten percent of what was collected. Instead of continuing to collect monthly, it dawned on me that with all these farmers, it would be easier if they just paid me once a year. The Oppios and all these people, I went out in the summer when they had money, and they paid for the year. I had that route right up until I graduated from high school. I'd deliver papers and I'd play in a dance band . . . .

Even with a car I didn't date too much. I ran around with girls in high school, but I could never get real steady, because what they wanted was to go out and dance and have fun on Friday and Saturday nights— nights when I was playing trumpet in a dance band. In fact, I never took a girl to a dance until my Senior Ball. Then I invited this gal and got her on the dance floor and discovered I didn't know how to dance! [laughter] But I'd watched a jillion of them from behind my horn.

Our band was the Winterettes, named for Darrell Winters, a music instructor at Sparks High who led us and played saxophone. Barbara Heaney was the piano player, and boy could she play! I was a pretty good trumpet player. Ken Bradley played the trombone. Our drummer was Croston Stead, the guy they later named Stead Air Force Base for. We played for a dollar an hour apiece, and we usually contracted to play for four hours. We'd play from nine until twelve, when they'd have a midnight supper, and then we'd play for another hour.

The Winterettes played every dance that they had at Sparks High School. Hell, we played everywhere: we played in Hawthorne; we played the Candy Dance in Genoa; we played all the dances in Fernley. We played in Gerlach when it was a five hour drive to get there. In those days the road was paved to Nixon, and then it was about a four hour drive from Nixon up to Gerlach on a bumpy, rocky dirt road. One afternoon we all crammed into a coupe, tied Croston Stead's drums to the top, and we took off. Got up to Gerlach about seven o'clock and played until the sun came up. At the scheduled end of the dance, we said, "Well, we've got to get going," and we put our horns in their cases and headed for the door. The dancers chanted, "More, more, more!" So we passed the hat to collect enough to play for another hour. (Often you'd get more passing the hat than you did for the first four hours.) And that went on all night . . . the sun was way up when we walked out of the town hall at Gerlach. Jesus, they loved us! And I was seventeen years old.

# 4

## *Being Snuffy*

THE NEWSPAPERS RAN a daily cartoon strip called "Barney Google," which featured a character named Snuffy Smith. One morning on my way to Sparks High I ran into my buddy, Elmer Nelson. He said, "What's going on, Snuffy?" It stuck. Everyone started calling me Snuffy. I had an old Model A Ford I'd paid twenty-five dollars for—bought it from some guy down on South Virginia Street. I painted a big outline of Snuffy Smith on each door.

A bunch of us decided to cut class one time, and we sped down to Carson City. We were showing off. We went over to Carson High, and, Jesus, they welcomed us with open arms! They bought us Cokes and said, "Sign the register." Boy, we were loving it. But when we got back to school we were met by Procter Hug, the superintendent. As soon as we had signed our names in the register they had called Proc and said, "You want to know where Smith and that bunch are? They're down here." [laughter]

I was always doing something. I went out for football, and the first day I got my front teeth kicked out. That was the end of me and football, but I played a lot of basketball in junior high, and I went out for the high school team. There were four or five of us who smoked (I had started smoking when I was fourteen), and Coach Tip Whitehead told us, "As long as you guys smoke you will never play on my A or B teams." He put us on the C team, but we beat up on everybody, and one day in practice we beat Tip's A team. "Don't make no difference," he said. "As long as you smoke you're not going to play on the A team." But we wouldn't consider giving up cigarettes . . . you know, a young kid, you can't tell him anything.

The big state rivalry in basketball was between Reno High and Sparks High, and Sparks High always had a real good team. For our rally before the big game, we'd have a bonfire. Weeks in advance we'd be collecting old tires and boxes and cardboard, and we'd build a pile of junk as big as a house out at the football field. We'd send guys down there to guard it because Reno High students always wanted to torch it before we could have our rally. So they'd come down, and one night they got in there and burned it up. We were so upset and so mad!

One of our guys, Benny Cironi, lived up Wedekind Road, way back on what we called Chicken Hill. His father was a chicken farmer, and he had a horse. We saddled up that horse and rode it over to Reno High's field, and we brought a plow along in a pickup truck. (In those days Reno High's football field was almost where Manogue is now.) Another bunch of guys went over to Reno High School with buckets of maroon and gold paint to decorate their building in our school colors. It started to rain, and we took that plow out of the pickup and hooked it up to that horse and plowed the biggest S you ever saw in your life right in the middle of their football field.

The next day all hell broke loose. Of course, we all stood around and pretended to know nothing about nothing. A couple of weeks later we got shown into the principal's office, and here was old Judge Cunningham, the municipal judge in Sparks. (Judge Cunningham's father had been a railroad engineer—ran a switch engine in the yards. When the judge was a boy he'd take his dad's lunch to him. One day he tried to jump up on the engine while it was moving, and he fell beneath a wheel, which cut off parts of both arms. His left arm ended in a stump above the elbow and he had a hook on his right arm. Scary looking guy.)

Judge Cunningham had twelve of us in the principal's office. He said, "It's all down. I know that you're the guys who did it."

We said, "Who, me? Did what?"

And he said, "Just don't give me none of that. I know you did it. Reno High's shop people have repaired the damage, got it all done, and it cost a hundred and forty-four dollars. Now you've got till Friday, each one of you, to come up with twelve bucks."

I said, "I don't have any money, Judge."

He said, "Then you're going to jail."

The next Friday we all showed up with our twelve bucks. [laughter] That's the closest, I guess, that we ever got to *really* being in trouble.

Of course, we were always sneaking a beer when we could. In the old days a lot of people made their own beer. My dad only made root beer—we didn't have alcohol in our house because of the Mormon religion—but by the time I was a senior in high school we guys would sometimes get a keg and have a beer bust someplace. When we wanted to drink a little and raise a little hell, we'd go up to the Wedekind Mine in the hills north of town. There were very few houses on Wedekind Road, and you could go anywhere up there. (We never drank around anyone's house.) Go down the canyon, down the other side of Vista, and some guy would have a keg, and we'd sit there and drink beer and talk and laugh and get foolish. On Admission Day we went down a little from Bowers Mansion toward Franktown, and up from the road there in the trees we busted a keg. But it wasn't like . . . you know, you only had maybe two or three keg parties a year. Now it seems like kids are drunk almost every weekend.

# 5

## *I Wasn't Planning to get a Degree*

I GRADUATED FROM HIGH SCHOOL in 1940. Until then I had never had a drink of hard liquor, but after graduation some of us went up to Tony's El Patio Ballroom and bought a bottle of whiskey for eighty-nine cents, and we went to the dance. At ten o'clock I was back home on my front doorstep, dead drunk. The guys were scared—they just sat me down on the doorstep and left. Mom put me to bed, and in the morning I woke up and thought, "I'd better act like I'm sleeping, because this is going to be . . . . " But Mom never said a word.

With high school behind me I hoped to make a career in aviation. Boeing, the big aircraft company, owned an engineering school and a flight training base in Oakland. If you graduated from their flight training program, you had a job with United Airlines; and if you got through their aeronautical engineering school, they guaranteed you a job with Boeing. I wanted to be an aeronautical engineer, and I had saved money for tuition, but I didn't have enough math to qualify for the Boeing program. So in the fall of 1940 I went up to the University of Nevada to get a year's math.

At the university I took algebra and calculus and not a hell of a lot more, because I wasn't planning to get a degree. I was recruited by SAE, probably because quite a few of the brothers were from Sparks, and I pledged with them. I also played in the band. ROTC was mandatory, but if you joined the military band, that took the place of it. So I joined the military band, which was part of the university band—when the ROTC guys were doing something, we played for them. Of course we played at all the football games, and my most vivid memories from my brief time on campus are of our 1940 team. We beat everybody that came to town.[1] It was just a matter of how much. I mean, like scores of seventy-eight to nothing! *Everybody* went to the games.

Our star player was halfback Marion Motley, a colored guy from Ohio who eventually played pro ball with the Cleveland Browns. I've seen him throw a football one hundred yards—stand on the goal line and throw it down to the other goal line. He was a football team all by himself, but he wasn't at the university to study. I took English from old Professor Miller, and

---

[1]  The 1940 Nevada Wolfpack finished the season with four victories, four defeats, and a tie. Of its first five games, all of which were played at home, Nevada won four and tied one, outscoring its opponents by a cumulative total of 240 to 12. The team lost its last four games, all of them played on the road.

Marion would come to class and sit at a desk in the corner and sleep. On nice days Miller would have the doors and windows open. Jim Aiken, the football coach, would walk by, stick his head through a window and say, "Hey, Prof, how's my boy?" And Miller'd say, "He's doing just fine, coach." And there was Marion, sound asleep. [laughter] Got a C in the course, a gentleman's C.

Midway through the season, driving back from San Francisco, Marion ran into a car filled with Japs out on the Yolo Pass, and some of them died. The California authorities had him up for manslaughter. On a Wednesday morning a meeting of all the university students was called out on the quad. Several professors spoke. Professor Puffinbarger got up and said, "We got a big game this weekend—we need Motley! We can get him out of jail for a thousand bucks bail. Now, there's nine hundred and eighty-two of you guys out there. You put in a buck apiece and I'll put in eighteen bucks, and we'll go down and get him paroled." And we did![2]

---

[2] A Solano County judge found Motley guilty of the reduced charge of negligent homicide, fined him $1,000, placed him under the supervision of the university for the next three years, and released him in the custody of Prof. Paul Harwood.

# 6

## *Brief, But Action Packed*

BY THE END OF MY YEAR at the university Boeing had raised
their tuition another five hundred dollars. My savings
weren't enough. Before I could go to the Boeing school
I would have to get a job, and the only thing in Sparks
was with the railroad. It provided a lot of work. Every
time you looked around, here would come another train,
and as many as a dozen engines at a time would be in
for service.

Sparks was a division point for freight and
passengers. It was where they put on the fast passenger
engines for the long run to the east—they'd go like crazy
out across the desert. Trains headed west stopped and
put on mountain crews to drive big, cabin-front Mallet
locomotives that were not so fast, but could pull right on
up and over the summit, even in blizzards. (Engineers
told me that they'd go over the summit in snow storms
so dense that they never saw a signal. All the way to

Auburn, and never see any cracks in the weather except when they were running through the snow sheds.)

My railroading career was brief, but action-packed. [laughter] I went to work in the shops as a wiper—that's the guy who cleans off the engines' rods so that the machinist can come by and see that there's no cracks in them and they're ready to go again. Then I became a hostler's helper. When an engine came off a run it went into the roundhouse, where it was serviced and readied and brought back out. A junior engineer or senior fireman would be the hostler. His job was to back the engines onto the turntable, park them in stalls, and then bring them out when they were ready. As a hostler's helper on the graveyard shift, I serviced engines going in and out of the roundhouse, eleven thirty at night to seven thirty in the morning till I almost couldn't hack it anymore . . . working all night, staying up much of the day, and then back to work again.

An engine and tender would be brought out, and I'd replenish the sand, and fill the water and oil tanks. In the dark, I'd signal the engineer that the job was completed by waving my flashlight up and down. One night I'm watering an engine, and I get the water done. Then I begin filling the oil tank, and I pull out the stick and shine my light up and down it to see how much oil is needed. The hostler thinks I've given him the highball to go ahead, and he moves out with the oil spout still connected. That oil is at about 130 degrees, so when it starts spewing, I take off. He pulls her over, and he has a gusher. [laughter]

36

That was nothing compared to the incident that ended railroading for me: A hostler would drive an engine down and put it in the roundhouse; then he'd have to walk maybe a quarter of a mile back out to collect another one if he did them individually. So he'd hook them all together and pull them down behind a lead engine. One night a hostler said to me, "Do you know how to run these things?"

I said, "Who do you think taught Casey Jones?"

"Well," he said, "go out and just put them all together. Release the brakes when you're finished, and blow the horn, and I'll drag them down here."

I got them all tied together except the last engine—it was 4204, a brand new Mallet. I reached up and cracked the throttle, and nothing happened. All of a sudden the steam hit, and the handle jumped out of my hand, and it was wide open! I slammed it closed, and hit the brakes . . . and broke the drawbar. Then I blew the whistle and come down off that engine.

The hostler's name was Dan Blevins. He said, "What happened?"

I said, "I think I broke the drawbar."

The roundhouse foreman came out to see what was going on, and I told him, "The drawbar is broken on number 4204."

"Did you do it?"

"Yep."

"You know the rules," he said.

I said, "You don't need an investigation. I'm leaving." I had worked in the Sparks shops for just a few months.

# 7

## *Avenger Pilot*

MY MOM HAD BEEN TALKING to our banker, and she told me, "Go down and see Mr. Sbragia. I think he'll give you a job." He did, and I was excited about getting away from that graveyard shift at the railroad yard. Finally I could sleep at night and work in the daytime. From wearing greasy clothes, shoveling sand and pumping oil, I went to a white shirt and tie . . . and even though banks were notorious for not paying much, my pay stayed about the same.

I started as a file clerk. The bank[1] hadn't done any filing on their loan reports for weeks. My first day on the job they said, "Here, file these." So I filed and filed until I had hangnails on all my fingers, and I bled and I hated it. I couldn't pick up anything without bleeding.

---

[1] The bank was the Sparks branch of the First National Bank of Nevada. See Appendix (pp. 203-210) for a discussion of operations at the branch in 1941-42.

[laughter] After that they made me a bookkeeper, and I posted the checking account ledgers. Then I started running batch sheets. The bank was kept balanced with these sheets—on one side you would list all the debits, and all the credits would be on the other. After I learned how to do batch sheets they started training me to be a teller. Finally they taught me to post the general ledger. I was moving up.

The bank was like a big family. Most of the staff were young, near my age. We'd stop off for a drink after work and we'd go out together in the evening; we'd play baseball together, go to the movies together, and get together with the girls who worked there. We were all great pals, and life was good.

Then one Sunday I was driving my girlfriend, Mary Margaret Cardinal, down to Gardnerville in my V-8 Ford to see her parents. On the hill south of Washoe Valley the engine began to rattle and clank, and then it just quit. A guy stopped to see if we needed help. I asked him to tell Pozzi's Garage to send a wrecker out to tow me in, and while we were waiting I turned on the radio. They were announcing that Pearl Harbor had been bombed. Soon all us guys were being drafted.

Everyone in Sparks knew when your number was up, and one Friday Chick Gazin, the head of the draft board, told me, "Well, you'll be gone Monday." "Oh, yeah," I said. "I'll be gone." I didn't tell him I'd already enlisted in the Navy Air Corps. Like a couple of my buddies, I had gone over to Sacramento to join the Army Air Force; unlike them, I flunked the written test.

I didn't even get to take the physical! [laughter] So I decided to go Navy, and I just took a train on down to San Francisco.

The Navy aviation selection board was in the Ferry Building, right there on the bay. I go up to the second floor and take the written exam, and I ace it. Then they start to give me a physical, and the corpsman says, "You know, if you're five-foot-nine, you've got to weigh a hundred and twenty-two pounds; and you only weigh a hundred and twenty-one . . . . " And I thought, "Jesus, I'm dying."

"Look," he said, "a street car stops out front. It will take you to Ninth Street, where there's a big grocery store. Go in and buy two quarts of milk and six bananas. At fifteen minutes to one, get on the first street car coming back down to the Ferry Building, and eat those bananas and drink that milk. When you get off, come straight upstairs and I'll weigh you."

I did what he told me, and when I got on the scales he said, "You weigh a hundred and twenty-two and a half. You're in!"

Not quite. The physical also revealed that I needed surgery to correct a problem with breathing through my nose. So the Navy gave me a deferment, and I got my nose taken care of in Reno; and three months later, back in San Francisco again, I enlisted. We all stood and raised our right hands and took the oath and joined the Navy.

Going into the war, the Navy had thought they might lose as many as twenty-five thousand pilots.

When they found out that they were going to lose closer to twenty-five hundred, they stretched flight training out, and gave us more and more classes, and made the experience more and more difficult. I went through twenty-six months of this! They kept saying that the pilots they were producing were going to be better trained, better qualified than the guys who were already out there; but in the end they never needed most of us.

For me, training began in the spring of 1943 with Flight Preparatory School at Cal Poly in San Luis Obispo. Four hundred of us were in this program, which gave us three hours of physical training a day and five hours of academics. We were the first to enter it. Before, cadets had gone straight to Pre-flight, and then into flying. Preparatory added six months to your training, and it enabled the Navy to stockpile large numbers of aviation cadets.

So many fresh recruits were coming in that they didn't have enough uniforms for us. We would wear slacks and sweaters into town on Sunday to see a movie, and the soldiers from Fort San Luis Obispo would taunt us: "Draft dodger! What's the matter with you, pal? Chicken shit?" [laughter] And there's nothing we can do: no matter what we tell them, they ain't going to believe us.

After preparatory training I was in a group that was sent to Ely, Nevada, if you can believe that! We took the Southern Pacific to Cobre, where we got off and waited for hours on the station platform until a Nevada Northern passenger train came up to take us down to

Ely. We trained there for about three months, and the situation was pretty relaxed . . . not much discipline. For a uniform we were issued some "pinks"—khaki pants that they had probably bought at Penney's or something. I mean, they just handed them to you and you wore them, and you wore a black tie.

The Navy had contracted with a guy named Kokendorfer to provide the flying service. He owned the airplanes, which were Piper Cubs, and he hired the instructors who taught us to fly. In addition to flight training, we learned aircraft recognition and "essentials of Naval service," navigation, math, physics . . . . Our physical training was led by an old athletic director at Ely High School named Dan Bledsoe. Hungry Dan . . . . [laughter] At the University of Nevada he had been an outstanding high jumper.

We lived in a beat-up old CCC barracks that had been relocated to the field, and there were communal showers and a mess hall. A Chinaman named Sim Tom, who owned a restaurant in town, ran the mess hall and gave us our meals. And there was a little recreation area that had a juke box big as a piano. Jesus, I will never forget it, because they played the tune so many times—Vaughn Monroe singing "Fly Me to the Moon." All night, every night. [laughter]

At Ely I learned to fly an airplane. Before taking me up for the first time, my instructor asked, "What do you know about flying?"

"I've never been in an airplane," I said.

He just looked at me: "You've got to be kidding. How did you get here?"

My instructor was a guy named Marty Kromberg. (After the war he started an agricultural flight training school out at Stead, and then he had one at Minden.) Kromberg was a great instructor, and I naturally took to flying. After only four hours of instruction he told me, "You could solo now, but they won't let you." In those days you were expected to solo at eight hours. If you didn't, you might get what they called "captain's time." You'd be put with your instructor for two more hours, and then you soloed or you were gone.

My day to solo finally came. Kromberg told me, "Now you're going up by yourself. No problem. Just remember that I'm 180 pounds that won't be in the airplane this time. It's going to take off quicker and land slower. Don't panic when it doesn't want to land!" [laughter]

I looked around. I wasn't used to that front seat, you know, and I looked around the cockpit; and then I look out and I can see the instructors standing down there, waiting, watching me. Oh, God! So I give it the gun, and up I go and make the turns, and I finally get lined up with the runway and start down, and all of a sudden it was like I had forgotten everything I knew . . . just bring it down on instinct and land the thing in a daze, and they come over and shake my hand through the open side-screen, and then I taxi the plane up to the hangar.

A bunch of cadets was standing around, and Marty yelled, "He just soloed!" They ran over laughing and shouting, pulled me from the airplane and carried me across the runway to a fifty-gallon drum filled with water, where they dunked me. I was elated, but I didn't go out and celebrate. It was just that . . . .

You know, there's something that goes on in a war. During World War II, the military couldn't handle the sheer volume of enlistees. Everyone wanted to go. We were mad: we were mad at the Germans; we were mad at the Japanese; we were just pissed off! A strange, exciting time, but . . . . December 8, Monday morning after Pearl Harbor, Benny Garrett and Bill Blake had enlisted in the Army Air Corps. Suddenly these buddies, two of my best friends, were gone, on their way; and both of them got killed. Screw it.

After soloing, I stayed on Piper Cubs for another sixty-five, seventy hours. Now we were doing more precise things. The instructors didn't say this, but they were really trying to teach us that an airplane was built to fly, and if you leave it alone it does a pretty good job all by itself. But you still have to make it go where you want it to go. They'd put you in a cross-wind situation above a road and say, "Fly down that road." And to do it, you're just crabbing along, almost flying the thing sideways.

We got to be pretty good fliers. They told us we couldn't do aerobatics in those Piper Cubs, but we'd take them up behind Mt. Wheeler where they couldn't see us, and loop them and roll them and do all sorts of things. [laughter] Still, we were just beginners. Over in Tonopah the Army had a squadron of pilots training on

P-39s, which were *some* airplanes in those days. They'd fly over to Ely and buzz our field before landing, and then get out and strut around, you know. We thought, "Oh, Jesus. Look at this." [laughter] (Many years later I got to know Chuck Yeager. Once while we were out duck hunting he told me that he had been one of those P-39 hotshots who landed at Ely.)

Our field was sixty-two hundred feet above sea level, and the performance of our Cubs was limited—they only had little four-cylinder, seventy-five horsepower Continental engines, which were breathing hard at that altitude. Climbing took time—lots of it. If you were going to practice spins, you took off and climbed for an hour; and then, right over the airport, you spun your plane and landed it.

Ely's elevation was so high that in the heat of the day the air wasn't thick enough to get much lift off the wings of an airplane, so we'd get up at four o'clock in the morning and fly until ten, and then we'd goof around and have lunch before starting our ground school classes. Our flying schedule brought us up against a Navy rule that aviation cadets had to have eight hours sleep each night. For us to get eight hours we had to be in bed by eight o'clock . . . and hell, there'd still be two hours of light left! So the guys would lie there in bed, laughing and joking and talking. No sleeping, but we were in bed. Sometimes for fun we'd slip out and chase jackrabbits at night. Twenty guys, each with a stick in his hand, would spread out in a line, and we'd run down a jackrabbit in about two minutes. They won't run straight; if they did, you couldn't catch one. But they'd go to zig-zagging, and when one cut away from you, it'd run right into another guy.

Weekends, most of us would go into town, but a couple of our instructors were from Reno, and they'd sometimes fly their planes home. Two of my friends flew back with them once—at Eureka they landed on the highway and taxied up to the gas station, filled up, took off, and flew on to Reno. As for me, my Aunt Vega lived in Ely, and I was a pretty steady boarder at her place on Saturdays and Sundays. She was always having a bunch of us in for meals, and we'd do our drinking in a bar across the street from the Nevada Hotel. Up the road, McGill was the site of a huge copper smelter, and a big open-pit copper mine was just a few miles out of town to the west, at Ruth. Ely was really a miner's town, just as wide open as you can get. Weekends were fun.

After three months training as aviation cadets at Ely, we were sent to St. Mary's College in Moraga, California, for what the Navy was then calling Pre-flight. When our bus drove on to the base, cadets leaned out windows yelling, "Jump off and run for your lives. They can't catch all of you!" [laughter] We were about to experience our first, honest-to-God, true regimentation. I mean, now they were going to teach us what it means to be in the military. The discipline was tough.

In addition to classes and drill, a big part of the regimen at St. Mary's was physical training to toughen us up and to prepare us for the rigors of flight. The Navy had put in eleven or twelve athletic fields, a huge gymnasium, and a swimming pool the size of a football field. After the war they left it all to St. Mary's, but the college just tore it down. They said, "We can't afford to maintain this."

Indirectly, the physical training program came close to crippling me for life. Here's what happened: The Navy ran the base sewage through a crude treatment plant, and then pumped it onto the athletic fields to irrigate them. Apparently bacteria in the sewage got into my left foot through a blister on my sole. One day I got up and my foot was kind of sore and stiff; the next day it was a little worse. Finally it hurt so bad I couldn't stand on it, so I went over to the sick bay. The foot was inflamed with a deep infection, so they sent me to the base hospital, where I was put on sulfa. (Penicillin had yet to be developed.) They'd give me half a cup of sulfa followed by two cups of soda as a chaser. That turned it to crystals, and when you urinated it felt like you were a sand factory. [laughter]

Days went by, and the sulfa wasn't working, and the infection kept getting worse and worse. My whole foot was red and swollen. One day my father showed up, unannounced. I said, "What are you doing here?"

Dad said, "Well, the doctor wanted me to be here when he talks to you."

The doctor came in and he said, "We don't know what this is. You got an infection deep in your foot, and we don't seem to be able to stop it. If we can't get this thing under control in a couple of days, we're going to

48

send you to Oak Knoll; they're probably going to amputate your foot right above the ankle. We wanted your father to be here with you."

I said, "You know, before this started I had a blister on the sole of my foot, from running or something. Could the infection have started there?"

He said, "Could be, but now your whole foot is infected and we don't know where the infection's centered. We'll look at you again tomorrow and make up our minds about amputating the foot."

I got lucky. By the next morning an ugly swelling like a pimple with a two-inch head had appeared above the arch of my foot. It was just as yellow as it could be. "Well," the doctor said, "now we know where it is. We'll go in and take care of that."

They wheeled me into an adjacent treatment room, and I heard the doctor say to the corpsman, "Go get some morphine. This kid's going to need some help." Then he said, "Never mind; we haven't time. We'll just go without it."

He came over to me. I was lying on a gurney, and he stood there with his gloves on and he had a scalpel in his hand. He looked at me and said, "Kid, hold on to the bottom of this bed—this is going to hurt like hell. You can call me anything that you want to, but we're going fix you."

He was right. It hurt like hell. [laughter] He lanced the infection and cleaned it out, and then he actually scraped the bones . . . with no anaesthesia. I started

49

getting well then, and everything turned out fine. I was second in my class when we graduated.

My next stop was Olathe, Kansas, where the Navy had its primary flying school. Athletics and ground school were secondary there; there was some class work, but it was mostly navigation, weather, code, the things you would really use from then on. And flying—you flew and you flew and you flew, Stearman N2-S biplanes.

Olathe is thirty miles west of Kansas City, out on flat prairie land. We were there in the winter, and between Canada and Olathe there was nothing to stop storms except a three-strand barbed wire fence. We flew in great big lamb's-fleece and leather outfits that made you look like you weighed three hundred pounds—you almost had to be helped into the airplane. On the ground you'd be freezing, but there were always temperature inversions—you'd get up to five thousand feet, and the air'd be warm up there, and you'd be sweating in that fleece jacket.

And boy, we flew! Before Olathe you knew how to get an airplane up and down, but they really taught you how to *fly* there. You did aerobatics and formation flying and precision landings. They had a circle that was a hundred yards in diameter, and you would fly down wind, shut your engine off, make an ess turn across the wind line and come back. When you came back you had to land in that hundred foot circle with a dead stick. They'd make you slip to a landing, too . . . slip it right down one wing and put it on the ground. And we did lots of loops, Immelmanns, spins, snap rolls and inverted snap rolls.

They really taught us how to make an airplane do what we wanted it to do, and the Stearman was one of the greatest airplanes I ever flew. You could do anything with it. You could turn it over on its back (the engine would quit then, you know) and fly it upside down; and then you'd kick the rudder and slam the stick forward, and that thing would do a half snap roll, and the engine would catch and away you would go. It was some airplane!

We were at Olathe for twelve weeks, and then they had a graduation ceremony and we were sent down to Corpus Christi, Texas, for advanced training. We were put into SNV's, the old Vultee "Vibrators," much bigger planes than the Stearmans. We did tons and tons of formation flying—what they called section tactics, division tactics—and more dead sticks into our flying field.

The Vibrator was the noisiest damned airplane in the world, and it didn't fly well . . . had bad stall characteristics. Our instructors kept saying, "Don't shut it clear off until you get it on the ground." For my first night landing I was bringing it down easy, and the wheels must have been about six feet above the field when it dropped; seemed like it dropped for ten minutes before it hit the ground, me waiting for the impact all the way. [laughter] Of course, all of us were used to full stall

51

landings. That's all the Navy ever taught—no "wheel" landings.

We graduated from Corpus Christi and got our orders. I had a very good record, had never had a "down" flight, and I thought I was going to be assigned to fighter planes. But I look up, and here I'm assigned to the naval air station at Fort Lauderdale, Florida, for torpedo bomber training. Well, at least I was getting closer to going to war. Skinner, my roommate, got the same assignment. We had six days travel time, and it only took two days to get there, so we stopped over in New Orleans for three or four days and drank a lot of whiskey and ran around the French Quarter. Then on to Fort Lauderdale.

Now we began training on the TBM Avenger, the airplane we were going to fly in combat. They give you a manual, and you read and you read. Then they put you in the cockpit, and you check out everything, and they blindfold you and ask where's this switch and where's that instrument, and you've got to reach out and touch them. The instructor says, "The Avenger's real heavy on the controls; you're going to have to use a lot of tabs to fly this airplane." And you say, "Oh, yeah, yeah . . . I understand." But you don't.

Finally one morning I walk in and the instructor says, "OK, Smith, you solo today. Go out and take number forty-seven." They don't even come out to the plane with you, but of course they're watching you like a hawk. I get my parachute and go out and climb into this thing, and sit there trying to remember everything. Finally start it up and taxi down to the runway and call the tower and tell them I'm ready to go. They clear me to take off.

I give it the gas and get up to full throttle, and the tail kind of comes up. I'm going down the runway at about ninety knots, and I pull back on the stick, and I can't budge it: "What the hell? I must have forgotten to unlock the controls." I'm sweating it, but about then the airplane just takes off and starts going on out. I think, "Well, if it wants to do that, leave it alone. I'll get it up high enough to where I can jump out of it." So I throttle back and put it in climbing power, and then I think, "I wonder if it really *is* just heavy on the controls?" [laughter] So I take ahold of it, and it's all right.

I made some turns, flew it slow; flew it in a dive; climbed it; flaps down, wheels down . . . monkeyed around and came back in forty-five minutes and landed. Landing an Avenger the first time was quite an experience—huge airplane, the biggest single-engine airplane in the world in those days.

When I got down everyone asked, "How was it? How was it?"

I said, "Oh, it was a piece of cake. Don't worry about it." [laughter] But that night I told Skinner, "That thing's really heavy, pal. I pulled on the stick and nothing happened. It finally took off by itself. All I did was keep it going straight."

We still hadn't been on an aircraft carrier, but we began practicing carrier landings—they painted the outline of a carrier deck on the field, and there was a landing signal officer down there to bring you in. You come over the perimeter forty feet above the ground, because that's how high you come in above the deck when you land on a carrier. You're going down through the trees, and it's frightening. The idea is to fly as slow as you can and get lined up and do a touch-and-go off the "deck." You just practice and practice and practice. Touch-and-go on that small a patch of ground is tough. When you finally begin landing for real, the landing hook solves lots of problems. You can make a terrible landing, but once the hook hits the wire, everything's fine. After many touch-and-goes they finally let you land with a hook once, and then the next time you use the hook you're landing on board a carrier.

They sent us up to Glenview Naval Air Station in Chicago to make carrier landings on the *Wolverine* and the *Sable*, two old passenger ships that'd been converted into carriers—old-fashioned paddle wheelers with flight decks grafted on to them. It was November of 1944. When we got there it had been snowing so long and so hard that we were far behind schedule. They said, "We'll never qualify you in time."

The following morning they took us down to the Navy Pier and put us aboard the *Wolverine*, and we steamed out on Lake Michigan before it got light. I had the flu so bad I could hardly hold my head up. Shortly after dawn ten SNJ's fitted with hooks appeared over-head. They were flown by instructors, who landed them

54

and started qualifying us. We all had to shoot eight landings. We went alphabetically, and it took all day.

While waiting to fly, we were required to stand in the catwalks and watch all the landings . . . shivering. My turn came at about two thirty in the afternoon. It was the first time I'd ever taken off from a ship. I took off and turned back toward the ship, and could barely see it through the snow storm.

The SNJ was a Navy conversion of an Air Corps trainer—it wasn't really designed to land on carriers. The hook was held up by what looked like an old clothesline wrapped around a post in the cockpit. When you went to land, you undid the line and let the hook fall down. On my seventh landing I dropped the hook and nothing happened; the barriers just kept rushing by. All of a sudden the plane jerked to a stop. When I got out I said, "Jesus, what happened?"

The landing officer said, "You broke your hook. We caught you with the first barrier, dropped it, and then pulled it back up and snatched you to a halt." He said, "You're qualified."

I said, "I only got seven."

He said, "You broke the hook. You're qualified."

After a week in Chicago they sent us to North Island at San Diego. We sat around for a couple of weeks before they transferred us to Alameda, California, into a Carrier Air Service Unit, CASU-6. Carrier Air Service Units were pools of pilots and crews awaiting assignment.

I was bored. I went to one of the F6F pilots and said, "You know, I'd like to check out in Hellcats." The Hellcat was the best fighter airplane in World War II if you go by its kill ratio. Its engine had a two-speed blower, and at altitude it was a very fast airplane. It was light, delicate, had boosts on all the controls—you just touched the stick or pedals and something happened. In contrast, flying an Avenger was like driving a big, cumbersome truck; but it was a neat truck. And at sea level we'd run away from Hellcats.

The skipper said it was OK for me to get checked out on a Hellcat. After learning the controls and instruments I took off alongside another one, and while we flew the other pilot talked me through everything and I got checked out. The next day I said, "I'd like to fly it again." He said, "Go ahead." (This was not the kind of thing you could do today, take a hot fighter up just for the hell of it. But in those days . . . . )

In training they had put us in pressure tanks, simulated a climb to twenty-eight thousand feet where they made us remove our masks, and then dropped us down to ten. This was to show us that if you lost your oxygen, you could get down if you knew what you were doing. I thought I'd see how it really worked. [laughter] I took off and went up like a rocket in the Hellcat, and up above thirty thousand feet I took my oxygen mask off and put the plane into a very steep dive. A minute later I was down to about twelve thousand feet. Everything was cool.

The next day I left to spend New Year's at home. I was sitting at the bar in a watering hole down on Virginia Street with a bunch of friends when my knee started to hurt. The pain quickly became very intense, and I knew I should get back to my base as fast as I could. Barbara Heaney, my old friend from the dance band, was working for United Air Lines. She got me priority to fly back to San Francisco.

By the time I got back to Alameda my knee was just killing me, and my ankle was so swollen that I couldn't get my shoe off. I was put in the hospital, but none of the doctors could figure out what was wrong with me. Finally they started reviewing what I'd been doing, and I told them about going up in the Hellcat and taking off my mask. They said, "Well, hell! Obviously you have an air embolism." It soon worked itself out, and I was able to stay with the guys when we got reassigned.

One afternoon early in 1945 my roommate Skinner tells me, "We got assigned to Air Group 13. It's been to sea once, and now we're going to join it for regrouping and training at some goddamned place called Fallon, Nevada. Have you ever heard of it?"

I said, "That's only sixty miles from home."

When we got to Fallon we really went huckley-buckley; we got with it; we knew we were going overseas from there, and it wouldn't be long. I was giving my all, and it paid off. When you regroup, each squadron leader flies with all his young pilots to decide who's going to be his wing man, and the skipper of my squadron, a guy named Ben Williams, picked me. I felt honored. It was quite a deal.

Much of our time at Fallon was spent practicing bombing and torpedo runs. For torpedo practice we were using Pyramid Lake, which is on a Paiute Indian reservation. The Indians fished on the lake, but that didn't matter. Hell, we were at war! There wasn't any of the commotion you'd have today . . . I mean, if we wanted to use their lake, go get it. Right? But our torpedo runs were done north of the center of the lake, to stay well clear of the town of Nixon down on the southern shore.

Our practice runs served a dual purpose: When you dropped a torpedo in combat in World War II, it wasn't on its maiden voyage—it had had ten drops before it ever got there. This was because early in the war the Navy had a lot of trouble with torpedoes. After they were launched they'd go straight to the bottom, or they'd surface and run erratically. One submarine even sunk itself. To get the bugs out of the things before they were sent to the fleet, the Navy began having each torpedo dropped nine times, with factory overhauls after the third, sixth, and ninth drops. After this, if a torpedo was still running hot, straight, and normal, it was then sent to ordnance, filled with torpex, and taken out to the fleet.

For practice drops, our torpedoes ran with only half a charge of alcohol fuel in their engines; and in place of the torpex warhead, they carried water with dye marker in their noses. A little pump forced the dye out as the torpedo was running. We would come down over the mountains around Pyramid Lake, put our Avengers right on the water, and zoom in toward the target—a three-hundred foot line between a boat and the buoy it was towing. (Three hundred feet was equivalent to the length of a destroyer.) We'd make our drops and climb out of there, while observers watched to see where our torpedoes ran—whether they were hits or misses. And we had to practice coming in at different angles.

When a torpedo ran out of alcohol it would surface, blowing out the remaining water and dye marker. That made it buoyant enough so that its nose, which was painted yellow, bobbed up out of the water. The boat would retrieve the spent torpedoes and return them to shore to be sent back to our base for refueling and rearming.

One day after we'd dropped our stuff on the lake, we flew back to Fallon and ran into a snow storm right over the base. The air officer radioed us, "Go out ten or twelve miles. There's a big dry lake out there. Land on it. And," he said, "I'm going to repeat this three times: Land with your wheels down; wheels down; wheels down!" [laughter] We flew out and put down on the playa and sat in the desert silence for a couple of hours. There was no storm or anything out there, only ten miles from the base. One guy monitored the radio, and finally he said, "It's cleared; we can go home." We fired up our engines, those big props spinning, and you should've seen the dust stream off that dry lake bed! Then we flew down to Fallon and landed.

59

(In 1994, out hunting doves with a buddy, I returned to the lake bed for the first time since the war. The Salt Wells "ranch" is out there on Route 50 near the turnoff. I told my friend, "You know, that whorehouse must not have been here the first time I visited this place. I think we would have noticed it.") [laughter]

We trained out of Fallon for thirteen weeks. Soon after that we went aboard the *Altamaha*, a Jeep carrier, and sailed to Hawaii, where we did everything except get into combat. We flew and we flew, and finally one day about noon, the war's over! Three years training and no war. [laughter]

Some guy said, "I hear we went up to Japan and dropped some kind of a bomb."

"Well, what did we do, sink Japan?"

He said, "No, but it was big."

I got back to San Francisco aboard a ship carrying troops and a cargo of sugar. As we steamed past Alcatraz I could see the prisoners over there. We anchored in the bay. They threw a Jacobs ladder over the side of the ship and lowered all our gear down into boats that came alongside. I went down the ladder and got in a boat and went to shore and reported to the separation center at the Sir Francis Drake Hotel and checked out of the Navy. And now, I'm a civilian. It was November 15, 1945.

# Part Two

---

*From Batch Clerk to CEO:*
*Las Vegas, 1946-1967*

# 8

## *I Wasn't a Batch Clerk for Long*

I WANTED TO KEEP FLYING. United Airlines had an office in San Francisco, and as soon as I was discharged I went down and talked to them. "You're a single engine pilot," they said. "We want multi-engine pilots, and they're going to be a dime a dozen." I filled out an application anyway, and then I went home to Sparks. But I didn't go back to the bank. Shortly before I'd enlisted in the Navy I'd gotten a fifteen dollar raise. After I enlisted, I told the bank manager I could be called up at any time, and he said, "Well, then, that raise won't make any difference to you, so we're going to take it back." That really pissed me off. When I left for the Navy I let him know that I didn't like him or his bank.

After the war there weren't enough jobs, and a million guys were out walking the pavement, looking. I didn't care—when the bank offered me my old job back, I told them I didn't want to work there. I didn't even want to return to the banking business . . . but whether you enjoyed your work or not wasn't an issue; in those days you enjoyed having a job. [laughter] I wound up back in banking, down in Las Vegas.

Transamerica, the holding company that owned First National of Nevada, had opened a small bank in Boulder City the day after Pearl Harbor. It was called the Bank of Nevada, and during the war it moved into Las Vegas. Claire Sutherland, the fellow who was running it, had been an officer at First National Bank in Reno. We'd known each other before the war, and when I refused to return to the Sparks branch, Sutherland called to ask if I'd be interested in a job with him. He said, "I'll pay your way down if you'll come take a look." And I thought, "Well, I've never seen Vegas, and here's a free trip." So I went down and got off the bus about eight o'clock, and by nine o'clock he'd sweet-talked me into going to work there. I moved to Las Vegas in November of 1945. It was still a little tiny town, fourteen thousand people, and the Bank of Nevada was a little bank.

I started as a batch clerk. I'd been away from banking for three and a half years, so this was kind of a refresher course getting me ready to go ahead and be a teller and chief clerk or whatever came along as time went by. I wasn't a batch clerk for long. The vault teller was a guy named Tom something, and I had only been there a couple of months when Claire Sutherland came to me and said, "Art, Tom's leaving. You're the vault teller as of right now."

I said, "Great, but I don't want to be the teller for the vault until I've counted what's in it. If I'm responsible for the contents, I want to know it's all there."

"Well, don't worry about it. It's fine."

"I *am* worried about it. I'm not running the vault until I've counted it."

"Look," he said, "I'll take all the responsibility for it."

About two thirty, just before we closed, Sutherland came back and said, "We got to count the vault. Tom has confessed that he stole twenty-five hundred dollars out of the vault and gambled it away at the Pioneer Club."

I said, "You remember what you told me: you'd be responsible."

He said, "I remember. I just want to be sure it's only twenty-five hundred."

So we shut her down and went in, and there was twenty-five hundred short just like the guy had confessed. But the attitude of people in those days was so different from now. When the Pioneer Club heard about it, they sent a guy over with $2,500 in cash. They said they didn't want any stolen money.

In those days every branch had its own vault teller. All your cash reserves were kept in the vault, and that's where tellers got additional money if they needed it. If they got too many aces (dollar bills) or fives or tens, they turned them in to the vault where they became part of the reserve. It was my job to keep the vault in balance; keep the tellers supplied with what they needed; take their excess off them.

As vault teller I also handled the deposits of the gambling clubs. We had the Pioneer Club, the Golden Nugget, the Sal Sagev—practically all the clubs downtown. Every day the Pioneer Club would send over two guys wheeling garbage cans on hand trucks, with a couple of guards. The garbage cans were filled with the Pioneer's deposits for the day. The guards would have a deposit slip, and you had to count everything again in their presence. It was time consuming, but we had a deal with all the clubs that we wouldn't count the aces. We would accept their count and send the bills on to the Federal Reserve, and whatever the Fed said, the clubs agreed to.

None of the gamblers, nobody in Las Vegas, wanted a dollar bill; it was almost immoral to carry one. Instead you walked around with your pockets being worn out by silver dollars playing around in there. [laughter] (In those days the silver dollar was the big old solid silver Nevada dollar. That was before they started minting pewter dollars, Eisenhower dollars.) So dollar bills would come in to the bank by the thousands. They'd just dump them on us and we'd send them back to the Fed. We didn't want them.

Very seldom would we get a bag of silver dollars in a deposit from a club; we just put them out. We needed sixty thousand silver dollars a week to service our casino customers. Silver dollars came in bags of a thousand that weighed eighty-seven pounds apiece. If you're a national bank, the Federal Reserve is required to ship you all your money, postage paid; but Bank of Nevada was a state bank, not a member of the Fed, and we would have had to pay for all this. The postage would have been horrendous. So we just got our big brother, First National Bank, to order the silver dollars for us.[1]

Whittlesea Cabs owned kind of a drayage company in Las Vegas. We'd get an old flat rack truck from Whittlesea, and go to the post office and pick up the coins. We'd throw those heavy bags on that damned flat rack, no guard or nothing, and drive to the back door of the bank. A Las Vegas policeman would come over on one of those three-wheeled motorcycles and sit there and watch while we carried the bags of silver dollars into the bank. There was no air conditioning then— everything was swamp coolers, which worked fine unless you had any humidity, which means they didn't work. By the time you were done you needed a shower.

I liked Claire Sutherland—he was a fun guy—but due to a bunch of little things, as time went by I got discouraged at the bank. I wanted out. I told Claire, "I don't know what's wrong, but something about this isn't good for me. I'm going to go back in the Navy." (To me, the greatest time of my life had been when I was in the service.) Claire said he wished I wouldn't leave; said things would work out. I tried to re-enlist anyway, but

---

[1]   The Transamerica Corporation, a holding company, owned First National Bank of Nevada (FNB) and had a controlling interest in the Bank of Nevada. FNB was headquartered in Reno, but had a vigorous branch in Las Vegas.

the Navy said, "Thanks, Pal. We got four hundred thousand guys just like you wanting to get back in." So I stayed with the bank, but I also started moonlighting other jobs. I had nothing else to do at night; didn't even own a car.

The night that the Golden Nugget Casino opened, I started working in their cage. I worked as a cashier for them on Saturdays and Sundays for the next five or six months—Harlan Sperbeck was the head cashier and I was his gofer. I was making more money per hour in the casino than I was as a teller in the bank. Oh, yeah! I even made more selling honey than I did working at the bank. [laughter] That's another story.

After I'd been in Vegas about a year I got a wire about the application I'd filed with United Airlines the day I was discharged. It said to report to Stapleton Airport—United wanted me. But I'd begun dating Charlotte Campbell, Claire Sutherland's cute secretary, and I said to myself, "Hell, I'm not leaving Charlotte; I'm going to hang around here." So I did. It wasn't that tough a decision; I was in love. [laughter] And all of a sudden things began coming together. I was promoted to assistant cashier, and now I was a junior officer, making loans; and another guy in the bank and I were kind of competitive, and we were both seeing who could go the fastest. Not on purpose, but just . . . you know how life is.

In the meantime my pal Sutherland took off and went to the Bank of America in California. (He eventually ended up on their board of directors.) I had met

Claire Sutherland when I was working for First National Bank in Sparks. He was a junior officer up at the First and Virginia office, and he would come over to Sparks to manage our branch while our guy was on vacation. In Reno there was an old place called Tony Pecetti's El Patio Ballroom. Tony had a band, and once a week they'd have a big dance over there. Before the war Claire was the saxophone player in Tony's house band. He was a real fun-loving extrovert.

When Claire went down to run the Bank of Nevada in Las Vegas, he was going to the right place at the right time. Vegas was a young, growing community, and he was a good banker who knew what he was doing, and he got the bank up and running. Generally he was a pleasure to be around, but he could be moody. When things weren't going well everyone was in his doghouse, no matter who they were. He also just loved girls, and he made no bones about chasing them; drove his wife crazy. But everybody liked Claire and we were all sorry to see him pick up and go to Southern California. Especially me. Now I'm sunk again; I'm without a pal. [laughter]

When Bank of Nevada was founded, Transamerica had a large position in it, but it was really started and developed and promoted by a bunch of important local people in Clark County. E. O. Underhill, Otto Underhill, the local Coca-Cola distributor, was the first president of the bank, but he wasn't a working president. Claire Sutherland ran things. When Claire left, Spencer L.

Butterfield became the general manager of the bank and eventually its president, but Otto stayed on as chairman. Then Otto got into a beef with Transamerica and he said, "To hell with it. I want nothing to do with the bank any more. I'll be a director, but that's it." A guy named John Weldon Wilson, "Weary" Wilson, who was the Shell distributor in Las Vegas, became chairman of the bank. Wilson ran the meetings, and he'd come down every morning and buy everybody coffee. That was the end of his banking for the day—Butterfield ran the bank.

Spencer Butterfield was loveable, but he had no goals or priorities. Hell, in the early days I don't think *any* of the guys at Bank of Nevada really had a vision of what the bank could be; of what direction banking should take in Las Vegas. I'm sure the bank would have grown at a more rapid rate if they had. Spence was just one of these guys who never rock the boat; everything's always fine. I remember once writing him a memo about an employee who was doing a lousy job. I wanted him to straighten it out, get the guy out so he couldn't screw things up anymore. When I handed Spence the memo he just stuck it in his desk, wouldn't read it. He didn't want any hassles. When the bank got to about twenty million, Spence said to me one day, "I hope it doesn't get any bigger." I thought, "Jesus . . . . " [laughter] I don't know. I was young and ambitious, and I was ready to go tearing down the road.

Spence was easily influenced. A young guy named Hank Greenspun came in one day and wanted to borrow a little money to start a new newspaper, the *Las Vegas Sun*. Hank had just gone through this thing where he'd been convicted of running guns for Israel, and everyone kind of looked sideways at him.[2] When Spence loaned him a little money, everyone thought, "You'll have trouble getting it back." But Hank wrote a glowing column about Spence; and about once a month he'd come down and borrow more money, and then there'd be another column about Spence Butterfield. This went on for a long time. Spence finally turned him down for another loan, and Greenspun got mad and wrote a dirty column about him and moved his account to another bank. He did eventually repay the loans.

I was the vault teller for about a year, and then I became the head note teller. That was a different side of the bank. In those days if you were making savings or checking deposits or commercial deposits, you went to a commercial teller. If you had to make a note payment on your automobile or your house or whatever, you went to a different teller who handled notes.

Commercial notes were something you hardly ever see now. The bank would loan Businessman X five hundred dollars for ninety days for a specific purpose.

---

[2]  In 1948, Herman M. "Hank" Greenspun acquired and shipped 6,000 tons of weapons and munitions to Palestine in support of Jews fighting Arabs who wished to prevent the establishment of the state of Israel. This action led to a 1950 federal court conviction for violation of several federal laws. Greenspun was pardoned by President John F. Kennedy in 1961.

He'd come in at the end of the ninety days and pay off the note with interest. Or the bank might make him a term loan, something like five thousand dollars repayable at four hundred fifty a month for twelve months. Note tellers handled these those sorts of things.

As head note teller I ran the note tellers and answered questions and kept them in balance. The position was also kind of like a "pre-assistant" cashier—I was a "gofer" for the lending officers, who showed me the ropes. One day after I'd been doing this for about six months they came out of the board room and said, "Hey, Art, you're an assistant cashier now. You're going up on the platform and you're going to make loans." I only got about a twenty-five dollar a month raise, but the promotion opened the door for advancement. Assistant cashier was the first level of an officership. That's where you start to learn how to discount loans, how to advertise loans.

In those days the loan officer took on all requests, including personal loans, and said we can or we can't. You didn't have clerks doing it like we do now—you did it yourself. You'd talk to a guy and try to evaluate him. You'd look at his occupation and his background and how often he changed addresses and that sort of thing. As part of my training the loan officer would have me look at simple loan applications, and he'd say, "What do you think?" If I said I'd make that one, he might say, "Well, I wouldn't. I'll tell you why." Or he'd say, "You're right, we ought to make that one." Unfortunately, the first loan I made went bad, which taught me some things. It was five hundred dollars and it was for a year, and the guy made about five payments and we never saw him again.

During the war thousands of Southern blacks had come to Las Vegas to work for Basic Magnesium and other war industries. The Westside, where they settled, experienced explosive growth. It soon became the largest black community in the state, but not many black people came to the bank asking for credit. If they did and they qualified, they got the money—our bank never discriminated on the basis of race in the loans it was making. The problem was, very few blacks were qualified to borrow, and the reasons had nothing to do with color. For instance, house loans: the houses that they lived in had no collateral value—I mean, the only thing of value about them was the lot that they sat on—and there was no way you could justify making real estate loans without collateral.

Oh, there were some blacks who could qualify for home loans, but, besides not having collateral that they could put up, by nature of their education most couldn't get good jobs. The average guy, washing dishes at a casino or . . . they didn't have good wages or job longevity or the sorts of things that indicate stability and a good credit risk. For a long time even our own government wasn't making loans over on the Westside. The FHA goes only where it wants to go—they won't go just any place—and in the 1940s and 1950s the FHA was not making loans on the Westside.

If you're an average lending office, and the government says it won't make any loans on the Westside, what are you going to think about making a conventional loan in the neighborhood? Nonetheless, Bank of Nevada would lend money to anyone who could qualify, and some blacks could. I personally knew a few who came in for loans, and I could check out the others by calling a businessman I knew over on the Westside. I'd say, "You know so-and-so?"

"Yeah, I know him."

"He wants to borrow a hundred dollars. What do you think?"

If the guy wasn't a good credit risk, he might say, "Well now, Mr. Smitty, I guess I *don't* know him that well. I guess we're talking about two different guys." But if the guy was OK, he'd say, "I'd trust him with anything."

I believed that if you made a loan you ought to be able to collect it. Once I had a delinquent loan and I went over to the Westside to collect it. Art Smith, bold young assistant cashier! [laughter] I rang and rang the doorbell, and I knocked on the door, and I went next door to ask the neighbors. No answer at either place; nothing. And it was quiet—nobody could be seen anywhere in the neighborhood.

As I'm getting in my car to leave, a guy comes driving around the corner and accidentally hits a dog that's out in the street. The dog lets out a yip and a squeal, and every front door on that whole block opens and people stick their heads out. *Everybody* was home, and they probably hoped I'd been run over. [laughter] It finally got to the point that we wouldn't let our collectors go over to the Westside because we didn't think it was safe for them. There was that much animosity. We would use a collection agency instead.

We got many of our lending ideas at conferences where you'd meet all the guys that ran the great big installment loan departments. In those days these guys were considered geniuses, and if you were lucky you got to talk with them. Some of them had begun financing ranges, refrigerators, vacuum cleaners, boats . . . anything that called for monthly payments. I got it in my mind that we could make some money with installment loans, and I finally convinced Spencer Butterfield that we should have an installment loan department. He said, "Who's going to run it?" And I said, "Well, I'm going to run it." [laughter] And I did. I did the bookkeeping; I bought the paper; I made the loans; and I collected the loans until we finally hired a collector.

We weren't going to make anything waiting for guys to come in and say, "I want a loan to buy a car." So my idea, which I picked up at one of these conferences, was we would go to the Chevrolet dealer and the Ford Dealer and we'd say, "Look, we want to buy your paper. You generate the paper, we'll buy it. We want to look at all your contracts." Well, we did that, but we were a little behind First National in Las Vegas, and when you compete in banking you can cut your own throat. You've got to make a better deal than the guy at the other bank, or the Ford dealer's going to go there. But you create a lot of smoke, and your name's around, and we actually did have a pretty successful department.[3]

In the early 1950s we put up a new headquarters building at Fifth and Carson. When Butterfield chose to locate it there, the guys said, "Jesus, why? It's got to be the worst location in the world."

So I asked him, "Spence, why are we moving over there?"

He said, "Any fool would know that's a good location."

"How would any fool know that?"

"Well, it just is."

But it was a lousy location. There was no foot traffic; there was nothing there. I wasn't there long either. I had decided it was time for me to be a branch manager, and I began pestering the officers: "When am I going to get a branch?" One day Butterfield said, "We're sending you back over to First and Fremont as branch manager." Boy, I went raring over, and I was so nervous . . . . An old gal, a secretary who had been there forever, finally said, "Sit down and relax, kid; everything's going to be OK." [laughter]

Soon after I became a manager the bank gave up on its Fifth and Carson location and put up a two story building at First and Carson, across the street from a

---

[3] See Appendix (pp. 210-11) for further discussion of lending practices.

76

mortuary. They moved my branch operation over there, and put the bank's headquarters upstairs. Now we had fifty by eighty feet right in the heart of the gaming district, which was good; but I don't think the location was calculated. *Nothing* was ever calculated at Bank of Nevada. [laughter]

Spencer Butterfield had been a good second man who got into his position simply by virtue of Claire Sutherland's leaving, and I don't think he was really qualified to run a bank. You always had the feeling that Spence's personal life was more important to him than his job—when he took over he had recently divorced and re-married, and he was terribly in love with his new bride, and maybe that got in the way. The board of directors seemed to be happy with him, but we have to remember what it was like back then—the board was not sophisticated at all. Earl Brothers, who was on the board, had the concessions at Hoover Dam, and he was a big entrepreneur. He owned the movie theater at Boulder City and the gift shop . . . hell, he ran Boulder City. And there was a fellow named Harrington, who was a big insurance dealer; and Bill Ferron was one of the largest pharmacy owners in Las Vegas . . . .

Spence had been president of the bank for about ten years when one morning as he was driving to work he came to a stop sign and couldn't control his foot to brake the car. The doctors discovered that the arteries in his neck were all plugged up. He was having trouble getting blood to his brain, and he'd faint. Nothing could be done. With medical care he got better for a little while, but then he had a relapse and was confined to bed.

One morning in 1958, when it was becoming apparent that Spence wasn't going to be able to continue, an emergency board meeting was called. The board meetings were held upstairs, and at about eleven o'clock Herb Greenfield, the bank's cashier, comes down and says, "Can you come upstairs? The board's having a meeting and they want you and me and Sutherland there." (This Sutherland was our senior loan officer, in charge of all the lending officers and responsible for all the credits in the bank. We called him Sully.)

We go up, and not only is the board sitting there, but also Oscar Keller, the president of Transamerica. They ask Sully and Herb and me to sit down at one end of the table, and they say, "We have a real problem with the bank. Spencer Butterfield is ill and we don't know when he's going to come back. We need some leadership, so we've decided to create an executive vice president for this bank. It will be Art Smith."

Well, my mouth flew open, and Sully and Greenfield looked shocked. They're both big wheels, and I'm just running the branch downstairs. Greenfield said this was an insult to him. Sully said, "I quit!" Keller told them he hoped that neither of them would resign, "but," he said, "we're not going to change our minds. Smith is now the executive vice president, and he'll be in charge until Butterfield gets back. There's nothing else to talk about. I'll buy lunch."

The board had probably decided on me because . . . well, Greenfield did what he was doing well, but his background was strictly like working in a tunnel. The head guy of a bank also has to be the community guy; he has to know people. Herb didn't know anybody, so basically he was not cut out to be the president of any bank. And Sutherland was quite a guy, had moved up rapidly, but he had an abrasive personality and had rubbed some people the wrong way.

I was young and full of enthusiasm when I took over, which was good, because although I was acting as president of the bank, I was also still running the branch downstairs. Finally we decided that I had to move upstairs, into Butterfield's office, because it had become clear that he was never coming back. In 1959 we made Butterfield chairman of the board and I became the president of the Bank of Nevada in title as well as in fact. I was thirty-seven years old. I had been making eight hundred dollars a month, and they didn't give me a raise; but I didn't care—I was the president! [laughter]

# 9

## *Take-outs*

THERE ARE THREE CLASSES OF BANKS: state banks that *don't*
belong to the Federal Reserve System, state banks that
do, and national banks. When the Bank of Nevada
started, they opted not to be a Fed member. But to
operate, you must have Federal Deposit Insurance—
nobody is going to put money in your bank if you don't.
It took a while, but Bank of Nevada finally got FDIC
coverage. That meant that every other time the state
bank examiners visited us, the FDIC guys came along.
They were tougher than the state guys, who sometimes
stood up for us and said, "Look, you're being too strict."
Walter Smith was head of the FDIC team; the state guys
called him "Missouri." They said, "He's like a mule. He
keeps saying, 'show me, show me!'"

All banks were required to set aside a certain
portion of their qualified loans in a reserve to protect
against possible future loan losses—in those days you
had to hold a twenty year average of your losses in

reserve. Bank of Nevada had only been going since 1941, so there was no twenty year average when I took over, and the examiners wouldn't let you use your actual loan losses for the year until you got twenty years. We had practically no reserves because we were using an average that was unreal and ridiculously low. But we never went through that reserve; we always had reserves left.

State banks could be a little more adventuresome than national banks in the way they did business. Real estate loans, for instance: the laws were far more liberal for a state bank—national banks couldn't make loans on undeveloped real estate, but state banks could. And permitted percentage of loan to value was much greater for state than it was for national banks. In fact, the rapid growth of Las Vegas in the 1950s and 1960s—the development of the Strip and big housing tracts and a variety of other things—was made possible to a certain extent by the two very active state banks in that community. Bank of Nevada and Bank of Las Vegas were able to do deals that First National couldn't legally do.

Bank of Las Vegas was started by a guy named Mattie Madison, who had run all the installment loans for the Bank of America. Then the Cosgriff group out of Salt Lake City, the Continental Bank there, bought the bank and sent Parry Thomas to run it. Whether by design or not, the Bank of Las Vegas soon found its niche with the gaming industry, and it became known as "the gamblers bank." From the early 1950s on, if you had a casino or a club, or wanted to do a gambling thing, you went to the Bank of Las Vegas and saw Parry Thomas.

Parry could make large loans to casinos because he had good "take-outs": he would put a loan on the books that he didn't have the capacity to carry, but he'd put it on temporarily and get it going and sell it to an insurance company or something. Obviously, two banks don't want to be competing for the same business if there're other markets, so Bank of Nevada went in a different direction. We were doing lots of residential financing—in a way, we were financing the housing industry in Las Vegas. We'd say to the builders, "Look, we'll finance your whole tract; we'll provide a home for the loan." Then we'd go to the insurance companies with that paper. I'd get ahold of someone like Ward Gay, an agent in the mortgage department of New York Life who'd buy the loans.

No one company had enough money to carry all the loans that were available. We were doing take-outs with Fred French of the Manchester Savings Bank in New Hampshire, with the Dime Savings Bank in New York City . . . there were about eighteen or twenty guys we could call and say, "Look, we've got a new tract, and it's going to be two and half million bucks. Do you want part of it?" It finally got to where we knew them as well as they knew us, and they got to where they knew the town. Ward Gay would say, "Art, is it a good deal?"

"It's a good deal."

He'd say, "Then we'll take a million and a quarter." It became almost automatic, and the insurance companies loved it. Insurance companies are different than anyone else. They know that they have to get a certain return today, and if they get it today they aren't going to worry about tomorrow, because tomorrow is a different number—they'll get that tomorrow.

We'd sell a loan to someone like Manchester Savings, and then we'd service the loan and make money on the service charge, maybe a quarter of a percent off the top. Manchester'd buy the loan at six and a half, and net six and a quarter. We'd collect their payments and see to it that the fire insurance stayed in force and the taxes were paid. (Once computers came in, you could do all this on your computer and it became a non-event. I mean, the computer'd say, "Hey, his insurance expired." So we'd write and tell the borrower, "Either renew the policy or we're going to buy some insurance for you.")

There's a tremendous capacity out there for long term debt, and we made a lot of money servicing take-outs. Banks don't like long term debt, but if they can make the loan, sell it, and make money servicing it . . . . They don't even have to tell you that they sold your loan to Fred French in Manchester, New Hampshire. [laughter] We made lots and lots of loans. I even financed the first Catholic cathedral in Las Vegas, the one out behind the Desert Inn. It was Father Toomey's project, but when you loaned to Father Toomey, you didn't loan directly to him. You loaned to the bishop, whose title in those days was "Bishop of Reno, a Corporate Sole." But Toomey gets the money and Toomey builds the cathedral and Toomey has to pay the loan back.

Moe Dalitz donated the land for the church, and there were some other large contributors to the project—Bob Keyser, an oldtime Las Vegan who used to run the DeLuca Importing Company, donated the baptismal room and font. After the church was open and running I ran into Father Toomey over at Bob's house, and he said, "Come up one night and see how things are going at the church." I didn't know that he held a mass at two o'clock in the morning for gamblers and casino workers, and I agreed. He asked me to pass the offering plate, and when I got through there was some currency and some silver, but the plate was just plumb full of chips. There was a twenty-five dollar chip from the Desert Inn; there were chips from the Sands; there were chips from every casino on Las Vegas Boulevard. Instead of the devout giving coin of the realm, they gave coin of the Strip. [laughter]

There was another bank in Las Vegas before the Bank of Nevada moved in. The old First State had been started in a grocery store in 1905 by John S. Park, but it had soon moved into a concrete block building at the corner of First and Fremont. For thirty years First State had a lock on all the banking in Clark County, and by the 1930s, with the huge payroll from the Hoover Dam project, it was doing a lot of business. Then the First

National Bank of Nevada, with headquarters in Reno, decided that they wanted to establish a branch in Vegas. Ed Clark, Jerry Crowe, Lee Ronnow, and Cyril Wengert were running the First State Bank, and they said, "We're not going to let you come in." So First National went and made a bunch of low-interest loans in Las Vegas out of their Reno office, and the guys quickly decided that maybe they didn't want this kind of competition. They sold their bank to the First National in 1937.

Transamerica, the holding company that owned Bank of Nevada, also owned the First National. When I started with Bank of Nevada in 1945, our Boulder City and Las Vegas offices combined had about four and a half million dollars in deposits, and First National's Vegas branch had about seven million. There were less than twelve million dollars total deposits in Clark County, and all were controlled by Transamerica.

While we were competitors with the First National, we were also brothers and sisters—from eight in the morning until six at night we'd kill each other, but after that we were buddies until eight o'clock the next morning. FNB being a bigger bank, they had bigger lending limits; so if we had a customer we were trying to take care of and we discovered that we were up against our lending limits, First National'd say, "Well, we can take care of your deal." They would help us that way. And when Eddie Questa, FNB's president, needed help he would come to me.

Although our relations with First National were good, we were still rivals, and sometimes the rivalry got a little foolish. Questa often came down to Las Vegas where he had a lot of casino business and some good friends. There'd be a fund raiser at the Sahara, and we'd give seventy-five bucks for something, and Eddie'd get out on the diving board and announce that First National was going to give seven hundred and fifty bucks. That was his way to put us down: "They gave seventy-five? I'll give seven fifty." Well, when you stop to think about it, the stuff we were doing was almost childish. But we did it.

One time Questa was doing some financing out on the Strip for the people who were buying Bugsy Siegel's old Flamingo. He wanted to make a loan to them, but there wasn't enough value there—by law a national bank couldn't include a parcel of undeveloped land that was part of the property—so Eddie asked me to bring in Bank of Nevada on the deal. (We were governed by looser state regulations.) I went out and financed that undeveloped piece of land separately, I think for $350,000; and Eddie was able to put together the loan on the improved real estate, and we accomplished what we wanted to do. The end of the story is that the borrowers didn't repay me—Eddie got free and our bank got stuck. [laughter] I had to foreclose, and we ended up with the damned land. But on the whole, the relationship between Bank of Nevada and the Las Vegas branch of FNB was one that benefitted us both.

## 10

## *SNIFing Around*

LAS VEGAS HAD A LOT GOING for it that would be good for business, like inexpensive power, good weather, no income tax; and in those days there was no sales tax. But when you were out of state and you said you were from Las Vegas, people would sneer and turn away, or they would look at you as if, "Are you real?" With the Strip and the glitter and the gaming and prostitution and that sort of thing, we had a big problem with our image. Then a group of guys came up with a way to sell Las Vegas around the country. They created the Southern Nevada Industrial Foundation, SNIF.

Bank of Nevada was a charter member of SNIF. When SNIF was in its infancy we gave a bank office to its director; just gave it to him so he'd have a place to work from. I represented the banking industry on the SNIF board, and there was another guy who represented the building industry, another who represented the big plants at Henderson, and so forth. Several times a year the director would arrange promotional trips, and the guys that were involved with SNIF would go and visit two or three cities. Maybe Dallas one day and Houston the next, and then New Orleans. We'd get the local Chambers of Commerce to send us a list of influential business people in advance, and we'd invite them to lunch. They'd come, and we'd say, "We have a little road show we want to put on. It takes thirty minutes. That's what you're going to have to put up with for a free lunch."

One of us would speak ("Las Vegas is a good place to live; it's a good place to visit; it's a good place to invest your money,") and then we'd open it up for questions. Of course, we steered away from questions about organized crime, because in those days there *was* organized crime in Las Vegas. [laughter] When the subject came up, our answer was that it was of no concern: "They're just trying to make a buck like everyone else." (The truth is, Moe Dalitz may have done more for Las Vegas than anyone who ever lived there. He might have been a bad guy somewhere else, but Moe really helped that town. And oldtimers will tell you that Bugsy Siegel's the guy who got Las Vegas going, put it on the map. His Flamingo Hotel-Casino was a radical departure from everything that had come before. Nobody called Siegel "Bugsy" to his face; it was always "Mr. Siegel" or Ben. He was a tall guy, a fine looking man, but I guess he was meaner than mean, famous for going ballistic every once in a while, screaming and hollering. When I was still a teller he'd come in to our bank to do business in his white shirt and black pants, with a .45 stuck in his belt. He'd walk around and talk to the officers up on the platform, then he'd come back to my window to do any money transactions.)

We went to Boston, we went to New York, we went everywhere. Parry Thomas and I always went, and sometimes Eddie Questa would join us. It was fun, and we met a lot of great guys, and by the early 1960s business people around the country started to realize that Las Vegas wasn't just a big gambling community with a bunch of girls in short skirts serving drinks—real people lived there. A big selling pitch was that we had more churches per capita than any city in the world. And it was true.

SNIF's promotion of Las Vegas helped us bankers in our efforts to find buyers for our local development loans. Parry Thomas had always had a couple of places that would take those loans—one was the Teamsters Union and one was an insurance company in Galveston, Texas—but there had been a long time when many potential investors would say, "I'm interested, but not in Las Vegas." After SNIF got active those attitudes began to change.

As Las Vegas grew, more airlines began serving the town. One night Delta Airlines threw a big dinner to celebrate coming to town—a Delta flight was going to leave every night at midnight for Atlanta, with a stop in Dallas. At the dinner I was having a drink with the president of the company, and he said, "You know, I wish there was some way that we could let the people in Atlanta know how important Delta Airlines is to them. Our headquarters is there, but we can't seem to convince them that we're a big contributor to their economy."

I reached in my pocket and pulled out a silver dollar. I said, "Some Friday why don't you pay all your people in Atlanta with these?"

He said, "What's that going to do?"

"Well, the first silver dollars that show up, someone is going to say 'Where'd they come from?' And your people will say, 'From Delta Airlines.' When your payroll fills all the cash registers in Atlanta with silver dollars, they'll know how big you are."

We took care of getting the silver dollars to him—sent out twenty bags a night on Delta's midnight flight to Atlanta until they had enough to make their payroll. A few days after our last shipment I get a call from the president of the Federal Reserve Bank in Atlanta. He says, "Are you the guy who sent all these silver dollars down here?"

"Well, I sold them to Delta Airlines."

"Do me a favor," he says, "don't let them have any more. The cash registers don't even have a tray for them. We're sick and tired of silver dollars; but they're still coming in by the thousands, and we have to turn around and send them to Fed L.A. or Fed San Francisco, which costs a lot of money. Please don't send any more silver dollars!" Delta had made their point.

The same thing with the Air Guard in Minneapolis. They said, "People don't know what an important thing the Air Guard is in Minneapolis." So I told them the same thing: send a couple of airplanes to Las Vegas, and we'll load them up with silver dollars, and you pay your people in silver dollars. They'll find out. And they did.

Eventually the treasury took real silver dollars out of circulation and substituted Eisenhower dollars, which were pewter dollars, wafers. Then came the Susan B. Anthony silver dollar disaster. People confused them with quarters. When they were going in, the government spent millions of dollars on a study that found that they'd be a total flop, and then went ahead and minted them anyway. We had three million Susan B. Anthonys in our bank for six months, and I think we got rid of maybe a hundred thousand of them. We sent the rest back to the Fed and they just melted them.

# 11

## *The First Computer in the State?*

THE FIRST COMPUTER that was specifically built for a bank was called ERMA. It was built for Bank of America by Stanford Research in the late 1940s. (It was a great big thing with thousands of vacuum tubes. Heat was a horrible problem.) The second computer for banking, a General Electric, was operated by First National Bank of Arizona, which was a cousin of ours through our holding company. I started to get interested in computers in the early 1960s. Hell, it wasn't just computers; by nature I'm a curious guy—if there's something new and unusual out there, I like to find out about it. I went over to California to see Al Zipf at Bank of America. "Al," I said, "I think I want to get a computer for my bank in Las Vegas, and I need some advice."

He said, "Yeah? How big is your bank?"

I said, "About twenty-five million."

He said, "Smith, I spill that much every day. I can't help you with that." [laughter]

So I went down to Phoenix to see Carl Burrow, who had put the computer in the First National Bank there. He showed me how their setup worked and gave me a lot of good advice, and I returned to Las Vegas convinced that we should have a computer. But the board of directors was skeptical: "Does Smith know as much as he thinks he does? He knows more than we do, but how much is that?" [laughter] They finally agreed to go along, and on Carl Burrow's recommendation we wound up leasing a big Burroughs 270. I believe ours was the first computer in the state.

The lease was just one part of the cost effectiveness equation, and we were initially a little apprehensive. When you finally get a computer on board, where's the offset in expenses? Of course, at first you run parallel systems. You take a branch and run it on the computer, but you also have bookkeepers working at night posting the statements and the ledgers to make sure that the two systems match up. Then after six weeks or so you're up to 97 percent saturation with the numbers, and you say, "OK, we're not going to post that branch any more," and you bring another branch on. Eventually you replace all those bookkeepers and night shift people and supervisors, and theoretically what you get rid of in the way of expenses is more than the lease on the new computer.

Of course, the lease wasn't the only cost associated with operating a computer: we may have freed up a lot of floor space that used to be occupied by bookkeepers and their machines, but now we had to construct a computer center to very special specifications. It had to be cooled because the early machines generated a lot of heat, and it needed quite a bit of humidity—so much that you could feel it when you entered. That was to prevent the accumulation of static electricity, which sends all sorts of dumb things to the computer. To house our computer center we built an extension to the second floor of our headquarters building—it jutted out over the driveway to our drive-in banking window.

We got the idea of using our computer to provide a service for the hotels and casinos that had slot machines: we would analyze and keep track of what those machines were paying every day. Of course, theoretically casinos could set slot machines to pay out whatever they wanted over an extended period of time. They could set them to pay out 90 percent of the take, 95 percent; but they never knew what they were *really* paying. Although it just required simple, tedious arithmetic, it would have taken a roomful of accountants to figure it out for all the machines; but with our computer we could calculate the average payout for each and every machine over any period of time, just like that!

The casinos would send raw data in to us, and we'd run it that night, and the next day we'd send them a report that showed what the machines were actually doing. There were immediate consequences. In those days gals were hired to walk around among the machines paying off the jackpots, and after we started monitoring the payouts with our computer, the Sahara

97

fired several of them because they discovered that there hadn't been as many jackpots as the girls had reported.

# 12

*A Lot of Fun*

CHARLOTTE CAMPBELL was the secretary for Claire Sutherland and later for his successor, Spencer Butterfield. Not long after I joined the bank we started dating. I went over to Charlotte's house one night, and her brother Tom was there and we got to talking about being in the Navy. It turned out that we both had graduated from flight school in Corpus Christi on the same day. I went and got my yearbook: here we are standing in the same picture, but we don't remember each other.

Tom was a real outdoors guy, and we spent lots of time together hunting and fishing. I can't adequately describe how good the fishing was for trout in the Colorado River below Hoover Dam back then; and you'd go up above the dam, and the bass fishing was . . . I mean, if you told people how good it was they'd think you were lying. One morning I was fishing way up Iceberg Canyon with a guy named Bruce Sutton. We were casting and catching fish, so we started betting two bits a cast. He cast thirteen times and he caught twelve fish. I mean, it was unreal.

I've always liked the outdoors, and in addition to fishing I hunted a lot. Quail hunting in those days was absolutely fantastic down around Las Vegas. Kell Houssels, one of the oldtimers, had a ranch out next to where the airport is now. He had a bunch of thorough-bred race horses on his ranch, and if you'd get way on the back end of the property and stay away from his horses, he'd let you shoot quail out there. So we'd do that, or we'd go and shoot quail down at Searchlight. The quail were so thick there that when they flew it looked like the whole mountain was moving.

I had been renting a room from a wonderful lady named Sylvia DeArmand, who was almost like a mother to me. Then Charlotte and I got married in January, 1947. Las Vegas was booming and housing was real short, so we rented a motel room that had a kitchen in it. (I'll tell you how short housing was: Vic Whittlesea, who ran for lieutenant governor that year, couldn't find a house in Las Vegas, and he was our neighbor in the motel.) We eventually found a house on Tenth Street and rented it.

While we were living in the motel I ordered some bees. First I ordered five hives from the Diamond Match Company, and put them together and painted them. Then I ordered five queens and five pounds of bees. (You buy bees by the pound.) I made a deal to put the hives out at the Stewart Ranch, which was where Cashman Field is now. They grew alfalfa and there was a spring down there, and there was also a lot of mesquite—mesquite pollen makes wonderful honey. Charlotte helped me. She had a smoker and a mask, and we'd go down and work the bees. An old guy named Silverman would buy all the comb honey we could provide him for his market.

Jess Myers, who ran the night shift at the Golden Nugget, got interested in what we were doing. He had a little four acre farm next to the railroad tracks off Charleston Avenue. And Jesus . . . he ordered thirty hives! So we build the hives, and I add my five to his. He says, "Now we'll have some bees." So we've got all the bees going, and he's got his wife working the bees, and man, we were raising bees like crazy. Charlotte and I did this for a couple of years, up until our first child was born, and we sold a lot of honey and made a lot of money.

After we were married Charlotte couldn't continue to work at the bank (in those days they wouldn't permit spouses or relatives of employees to work there), so she left and got a job with Pioneer Title Insurance. She typed title policies for quite a while, and then the president of the company, a guy named M. M. Sweeney, Major Minor Sweeney [laughter], married his secretary. Pioneer's nepotism rule kicked in and Charlotte became Sweeney's personal secretary. When we had our first child Charlotte became a full-time mother. By then, to make a little extra money I was keeping three sets of books on the side—a golf pro's, a concrete supply company's and a used car dealer's.

Our daughter Barbara was born in 1949. A couple of years later we had saved some money, and I had a Veterans Administration loan, and we built our first house. It was at Fifteenth and Sweeney Streets, which was right on the edge of the desert then. (Now it's in the middle of town.) It was so far out that they hadn't even extended the water mains that far when we moved in. Two blocks away there was a subdivision that did have water, so I went down and asked a guy if I could put a hose on his faucet to bring water up to our house. (In those days, there were no water meters or anything.) He said to go ahead, so I hooked a bunch of hoses together and we had water. The only problem was that with the hose lying out in the summer sun, the water would get so hot that you'd have to let it run for about ten minutes before it cooled enough so that you could take a shower. We had that setup for two or three months, and then they got the water mains in.

We lived there for quite a while, and then we moved way down on South Sixteenth Street. In the meantime our other three children had been born—Debbie in 1953, Arthur M. III in 1955, and Blake in 1959. My life didn't change too much after we started having kids. Charlotte has always been . . . she's Mom, and she takes care of the kids; and if I wanted to go fishing, she'd say, "Go and have a good time." None of this, "Look, I tended them all week. It's your turn to tend them on Saturday and Sunday!" I didn't get restricted that much.

When I discovered golf, it almost became an obsession. One of my very best friends in Las Vegas was Jim Cashman. (His father was a real oldtimer, helped settle the town.) Jim started playing golf and saying what a wonderful game it was. I said, "That's the phoniest game in the world. For Christ's sake, you just tee up that white ball and see how far you can hit it. Don't make any sense."

Well, we argued for a while and he said, "I know about you—you've tried golf and can't play it, so you just won't admit that it's a great game."

I said, "I've never had a golf club in my hands."

He said, "I'll bet a brand new set of clubs that you can't learn to play the game."

In those days Las Vegas only had nine holes, the old municipal golf course. I called up about lessons, and the pro said, "Come on out." So I go out there and take my tie off, and I walk in and say, "I'm Art Smith."

He says, "Where's your clubs?"

"I don't have any clubs."

"Well," he said, "we'll start with one of mine." He took out a seven iron, and he said, "Where's your shoes?"

I said, "I got them on." [laughter]

He said, "You got to have golf shoes."

"Why?"

"Well," he said, "because you . . . well, we'll give you a lesson anyway." He said it was so much a lesson and so much for six, and I said, "I better take six."

103

After my first lesson I took a pair of street shoes down to a shoemaker and had him put some spikes in them for me. Then I went over to Firestone and bought a dinky old set of five clubs. I practiced five times between each lesson, and the pro told me if I stayed with it I could become a pretty good golfer. I could see this, so I signed up for four more sets of lessons. Even though I still hadn't played a round of golf, I was hooked.

I'd hit them goddamned golf balls all afternoon, go home, and Charlotte would say, "Where you been? You're working too hard." I'd say, "You know where I'm working? I've been at the driving range hitting golf balls." [laughter] Eventually she was going to find out anyway.

One day I was practicing, and Herb McDonald and young Ike Houssels came by and said, "You want to play golf today?"

I said, "God, I've never been on the golf course." So I went to the pro and I said, "John, can I play?"

He said, "Bring your bag over here." By that time Cashman had bought me a good set of clubs. John took out the driver and the wedge and the nine and two irons. He said, "Go play."

Thirty-six par, and I shot thirty-eight. Next time I parred the course. I thought, "Hell, there's nothing to this." Then about three weeks later I shot fifty-two or something, and I knew that it wasn't going to be that easy.

Golf almost consumed my life for a while; all I could think of was golf, golf. If I had been on the golf course and learned that my house was on fire, I'd have said, "Well, I'll be there as soon as I finish this round." [laughter] That was when I was an assistant branch manager. Then I became a branch manager, and I didn't have the time. I still played every Saturday and Sunday and on the holidays, and it was never a problem at home: "You go play golf, and I'll tend the kids."

I also flew a lot. With the GI Bill I took some supposed flying courses. I could fly better than the instructor, but all I was interested in was the use of the airplane. We'd fly up to Mesquite to shoot quail. The sheriff would meet us at the landing strip in his pickup, and he'd let us take the truck. We'd go out and shoot quail and come back and get in the airplane and fly back to Vegas.

I finally got my multi-engine license and instrument rating, and after I became president of Bank of Nevada I bought a half interest in a Cessna 320, which was a twin engine turbocharged airplane that carried a pilot and four passengers. The turbos on the engines gave them more horsepower at a higher altitude than the standard Cessna 310, and you could go right up to twenty thousand feet if you put oxygen on. Charlotte and I would put all four kids in that thing and we'd fly to Montana or over to Caliente or wherever we wanted to go. We did a lot of flying in that twin, and we had a lot of fun together.

"My parents' marriage worked almost as if it had been planned." Elva and Arthur M. Smith, 1956.

On the Knudson farm near Brigham City, Utah, 1925. Art is astride the horse, his Uncle Edgar is on the right, and his father holds little brother Bobby.

"Hell, we played everywhere." The Winterettes, 1938. From left to right: Croston Stead, Bill Curry, Art Smith, Darrell Winters, Barbara Heaney.

"It was 4204, a brand-new Mallet. I reached up and cracked the throttle, and nothing happened. All of a sudden the steam hit . . . ." Southern Pacific 4204 in the Sparks yard, 1939.

"Finally one morning I walk in and the instructor says, 'OK, Smith, you solo today. Go out and take number forty-seven.'" Art climbs into the cockpit of a TBM Avenger.

"I went home to Sparks, but I didn't go back to the
bank." Art with his mother and sister Margery after his
discharge from the Navy.

The presidents of the four largest banks in Nevada, 1962. Left to right: Don Bates, Nevada Bank of Commerce; Eddie Questa, First National Bank of Nevada; Art Smith, Bank of Nevada; and Parry Thomas, Bank of Las Vegas.

"Reluctant though we had been, once FNB decided to issue a credit card we just promoted the hell out of it." Art and Harold Gorman, 1968.

"In 1981 FNB became First Interstate Bank of Nevada. Nothing changed except our name, but we made a big deal of it. We had all new signs up, and they were draped, and everyone went out in front and I yanked the cord and we became First Interstate Bank."

"In a life filled with good fortune, my greatest luck was to have Charlotte for my wife."

# 13

## *Mormons and Masonry*

BEFORE I MARRIED CHARLOTTE, her brother Tom married Virginia Mathews, a Mormon gal from Panaca. When Tom decided to convert Virginia to Catholicism, Charlotte said, "While you're at it, I want to convert Art." Along with a close friend who had a wife who wasn't Catholic, we all started going down to Father Crowley's parish to take instructions. We did that for a long time, but he didn't get any of us.

When we were finally ready to marry we went to Father Baldus. He said that if I accepted Charlotte's beliefs and agreed to allow any children we had to be raised in her faith, he'd go ahead and marry us even though I wasn't a Catholic. Well, I was in love. I told him, "Of course I will." I meant it at the time; but when Barbara was born I kind of got my dander up, and I said, "You know, Char, I don't see why I have to predetermine what my kids are going to be religiously. That's wrong.

To heck with it; I'm not going to insist that she become a Catholic."

Charlotte said, "I don't care what she is, but she's going to have a religious education. If you want me to give it to her, I'll take her to the Catholic church. If you don't want me to do it, you take her some place."

And I said, "Mom, you win." [laughter]

Hell, I didn't go to any kind of church. I'm just not religious. I was raised a Mormon, but I definitely don't believe in Mormonism. If you're a Mormon, that's all there is: You're a Mormon, and all you do is Mormon; it's your life. I'm not ready for that. The other side of the coin is that nobody takes care of their own better than Mormon people. I know that even though I don't go to church, if something real bad happened to me today, tomorrow my home would be full of Mormons trying to help. You never want to give that up; but it's just real hard for me to believe that a guy went out in the hills and dug up some gold plates, and an angel sat on his shoulder and transcribed them for him. And the stories about Joseph Smith . . . I don't know; he may have been a Mason.

The Masons have a certain sign that you make if you are in real distress—if another Mason sees it, he's obligated under oath to help you. When the mob got ready to string up old Joseph Smith there in Nauvoo, Illinois, he made the secret sign four times, but all the Masons in the crowd turned their heads, didn't want to see it. I've also been told that up where the Apostles meet in the Mormon temple, things are set up just like

108

a Masonic Lodge—that the Apostles even wear little aprons like Master Masons, except theirs are green. I see some other parallels between Mormonism and the Masons: women can't be Masons, and until recently women had no authority or status in the Mormon church; Masonry excludes black people, and blacks had no status in the Mormon church until recently. There are similarities.

Sometime in the late 'fifties, when I applied to join the Masons, their membership chairman came to see me. He said, "You got a problem: you're a Catholic. There's a conflict between Masonry and Catholicism. Catholics believe that you confess everything, and there are vows that we are going to ask you to take in the Masonic temple that you can't tell anybody."

"Well," I said, "I'm not a Catholic. I did take Catholic instructions, but I didn't join the church." Bruce Sutton was a very strong Mason; he got me in. We used to go up to Springfield, Utah, to shoot pheasants back when they were thicker than starlings on a dairy farm.

# 14

*Nukes*

TED WIENS WAS A SUCCESSFUL businessman, had the
Texaco and Firestone distributorships in Las Vegas. He
and I were going fishing in the Colorado River down
below Hoover Dam one morning. We got up real early to
drive out there, and it was still dark when we started
across the dam. Suddenly the sky just went pure white.
You could see clear up Lake Mead, see all the different
colors of the rocks and everything. Then it started going
down and getting dimmer, dimmer; and finally everything got dark.

Wiens turned to me and said, "What the hell was
that?"

I said, "Jesus, I don't know. All that light! Do you
think a fuse or a generator or something blew . . . ?"
Boy, what a deal.

We drove across the dam, went on down to Willow
Beach and fished all day. Driving home we turned on the
radio and learned that they'd exploded an atomic device

that morning over the desert north of Las Vegas. It was the first at the Nevada Nuclear Test Site.

There had been no announcement in advance, but I'd had a clue that something might be going on out there in the desert. John W. Wilson was an old mining engineer who'd been the president of my bank's board of directors. (His nickname was "Weary" Wilson.) He'd kind of taken a shine to me. Wilson was a prospector at heart, and one day he told me that he'd found some black opals in the desert up to the north. He said, "You haven't seen anything like this. One of these Sundays you and I are going to get in the car and go out and find some more." Two or three weeks later he came by to tell me we couldn't go looking for the opals: "Billy Ogle was in town, and I was telling him about where I found them, and he said you can't get in there any more. The government won't let you." And that was the end of that.

(Dr. William Ogle was in charge of the nuclear testing program, but he was still just "Billy" to everyone. He'd grown up in Las Vegas, graduated from Las Vegas High School and gone on to become a physicist . . . and the first inkling we had that something big could be about to happen was when Billy said we couldn't go out to look for black opals.)

Later I would visit the nuclear test site with my friend, Ralph Leigon, the head of the Electricians Union in Las Vegas. He had a big work force on the site. I'd ride with him, or he'd fix it for me to go up with someone, and I'd get through the security gate at Mercury that way. Once during the early testing of atom bombs, the government brought in a bunch of important journalists to witness the detonation of one. I joined the group, and we went up on a little ridge which was called the "news knob." There must have been a hundred of us sitting there, waiting expectantly. Pretty soon the guy on the PA system announces that the airplane carrying the bomb is over Kingman, Arizona, on its way to the test site. Some time passed, and then he said, "It's over Hoover Dam." Then he announced that the airplane was over Las Vegas; then that the bomb bay doors were open. Then, "Bomb is away."

They dropped the bombs on parachutes in those days, and the guy began the countdown a minute before detonation. Soon he was saying, "Forty seconds . . . thirty seconds . . . " We'd been issued smoked, dark glasses, and he said, "Pull your goggles down over your eyes and keep them there until we tell you to remove them." Then he said, "Twenty seconds . . . ten, nine, eight, seven, six, five, four . . . " I was sitting next to Lowell Thomas. When the announcer counted "three," Thomas said "Oh, shit!" [laughter] Three seconds till the moment of truth, and he was thinking, "I wish I wasn't here."

When the device went off I felt the heat before I heard or saw anything. We were maybe five miles away from where it went off, but it was just like getting sunburned. I could feel that terrific heat; then I heard the explosion and felt the wind, and it seemed like it went on forever. Finally the guy said, "You can take off your goggles and look now." We took our goggles off, and by that time the big cloud was building and it looked like a fire that would never go out. You wondered, "How are they ever going to get this thing to stop?" But it finally did.

# 15

---

## *Visiting With Mr. Hoover*

J. EDGAR HOOVER came to Las Vegas to speak at an American Legion convention, and for some reason he wouldn't stay at any of the hotels on the Strip; absolutely would not. I suspect that he thought there were still some Mafia connections there. Dean Elson was the FBI guy in charge. We were friends, and he came to me and said, "We got a problem. Mr. Hoover is not going to stay at a hotel on the Strip. Do you have any ideas?"

We had an auditor at the Bank of Nevada who was married, but had no children. He lived about a block from me. I told Dean, "What if we can get this fellow to move out? Would Hoover stay in his home?"

Dean got back to me and said, "He would like that."

So I went to this fellow and I told him what the deal was, and I said, "How would you like to spend four days in the best suite at the Desert Inn?"

He said, "Sure, I'll do that." So we arranged that he would move out and J. Edgar Hoover and whoever travelled with him in the way of security would have that house.

About a week before Hoover arrived Dean Elson came to me and said, "He needs a car while he's here."

I said, "Well, I got this new Cadillac."

"Could we borrow it?"

I said, "Of course."

He said, "But we need it three days before he gets here." I wonder what that's all about, but I'm not going to ask—I'm sure that they put radios and everything else in there. So Hoover used my Cadillac while he was in Las Vegas, but when he left I didn't get the car back for four days.

While he was there a personal invitation came. Mr. Hoover wanted me to attend a little reception he was having in one of the suites at the Sahara. I had no idea what was in store, but I went out there and got in the elevator and the operator pulled out a badge. He was FBI, and he said, "Can I have your name, please?" I said, "I'm Arthur M. Smith," and he looked at his list and said OK and took me up to the room. I walked in and Mr. Hoover was there and his assistant director, Clyde Tollson, was there. The only guy from Nevada other than me was Milton Prell, who was one of the owners of the Sahara. George Meany, the head of the AFL-CIO was there, and Jack Warner was there from Warner Brothers. You couldn't believe it.

The just-retired governor of Ohio was there; I'd never heard of him. I have the Legion of Honor from the

DeMolays, and I had their ring on, and he looked at it and said, "You're one of those guys, too, huh?"

I said, "Yeah. You know what that is?"

He said, "I got one just like it." There's not too many Legionnaires in the DeMolay.

It was really a funny reception. I don't think there were a dozen people there—and no women. You sat and visited, and Hoover just stood and talked, and you had a drink and you left.

Hoover and I corresponded for a while after that. When he replied to my first letter he wrote to the "Honorable Arthur M. Smith." Then the next time the salutation would be "Dear Honorable Smith." Then I got a letter one day that starts "Dear Smith." I knew Deke De Loach, an FBI assistant director in charge of criminal records, so I called him up and said, "Hey, what did I do to make Hoover mad?"

He said, "What do you mean?"

I said, "Jesus, he used to write to me Honorable Arthur M. Smith, and now I'm just Smith."

He said, "You've arrived! When he calls you just Smith, you're part of his inner circle."

I continued to see Hoover every now and then. I was at a bank convention in Washington, D.C., sitting around the bar one night, and four or five of the wives were there with my wife, and they said, "What can we do tomorrow?"

I said, "You ought to go over to the FBI laboratories and take a tour. They'll show you everything. They'll even let you shoot a gun down in the firing range. You'll really enjoy it."

They said, "That might be fun."

I'd had a drink, and I said, "As a matter of fact, how would you like to meet J. Edgar Hoover? I'll fix it up for you."

They all said, "Oh, gee whiz!"

The next morning I woke up and I thought, "Jesus, what have I done? How will I get this straightened out? I hope Hoover's out of town." [laughter]

I called Deke De Loach and said, "Hey, I talked a little bit too much last night, Deke, and I told these gals that they could meet J. Edgar Hoover. Is there any chance that he would give them five minutes?"

He said, "I don't know." But he phoned me back in a little bit and said, "Be here at ten thirty."

It was really cute. We walked in and De Loach took us to one of the secretaries, and he said, "This is Mrs. Bob Bryan and this is Mrs. Art Smith and this is Mrs. Ralph Voss . . . there were five of them. Then we were escorted to Hoover's office. An FBI agent was outside the door, and another one was inside. Both were black, and both were very sharp.

We had walked into an office the size of a long banquet hall. Down at the end was Hoover's desk. Three pictures were on the wall: one of the president, one of the attorney general, and one of the inspector who had been killed on the raid on Pretty Boy Floyd. As we came through the door Mr. Hoover got up from his desk, which was probably fifty paces away, and started walking up. He said, "Good morning Mrs. Bryan, it's nice to meet you." And he turned and said, "Mrs. Voss, how are things in Oregon?" And he said, "Mrs. Smith, how do you do?" These women's mouths just flew open—how did he know which one was which? He visited with us for a few minutes and then we left.

The next time I was in J. Edgar Hoover's office I was in the company of the governor of Nevada. I had first met Paul Laxalt on a basketball floor when I was playing for Sparks High School and he was playing for Carson. Later in life I supported him in his campaign for governor. About the time Paul was running for election, the FBI put wire taps on some phones in Las Vegas. When this came out Governor Grant Sawyer raised all sorts of hell with J. Edgar Hoover and the government for making illegal wire taps. They probably *were* illegal, but one of Paul's campaign promises was that he would make peace with Hoover and the FBI if he was elected governor.

After Paul was elected he called Washington a couple of times and tried to make an appointment to meet Hoover. They said, "The director is busy."

"But this is the governor of the state of Nevada."

"The director doesn't meet with the governor of every state in the union."

Since I'd met Hoover a couple of times, and I knew Deke De Loach, I called Deke and told him, "The governor really wants to mend the fence. He wants to get to know the FBI better and to extend an olive branch." De

Loach said he'd see what he could do, and he called back later to say, "I'll give you three dates. The governor can have any one of them and Mr. Hoover will be happy to visit with him, but once he picks a date he can't change it." We picked the date, and Paul and his brother French [Robert Laxalt] came down to Las Vegas, and we all got on an airplane and flew to Washington to meet J. Edgar Hoover. We spent a whole morning with him. The governor conveyed that he was a reasonable guy and wanted to do a good job as governor, and that he wasn't going to play games with the FBI. He was sorry for what had happened under the previous administration, and can we be friends?

I think a lot of good came of that meeting, but I didn't help things any. As we were talking along Hoover said to Laxalt, "Do you know who owns Caesar's?"

Laxalt said, "I think so."

Hoover said, "I'll tell you who owns three quarters of it: a guy named Raymond Patriarch who runs the mob in Providence, Rhode Island."

Dummy me, I said, "Can you prove that?"

Hoover said, "Sure I can."

I said, "Then why don't you do something about it?"

He said, "I'd lose two of my best informers if I did, Mr. Smith."

"Oh."

# 16

*Benny Binion's*
*Ten Thousand Dollar Bills*

JOE BROWN WAS OUT OF Biloxi, Mississippi. He'd been gaming all his life, but never where it was legal until he bought the Horseshoe Club from Benny Binion when Binion had to go to jail. One day Brown came into the bank and said, "I want a million dollars in ten thousand dollar bills." It was for a publicity stunt—he was going to put them on a panel at the casino so people could walk in and get their picture taken standing alongside a million dollars. Fine! So I called up the Federal Reserve, Los Angeles. The guy who was running it was a Canadian by the name of Volberg. I says, "Mr. Volberg, I need a million dollars in ten thousand dollar bills."

"Well," he says, "you can't have a million dollars in ten thousand dollar bills. We don't want them out there in circulation."

I say, "I have a customer that wants them. Is there a law against it?"

"No. But does he understand what the shipping charges and insurance would be on them?"

"Mr. Volberg, the thought of insurance never entered his mind and it never will. He just wants a million dollars in ten thousand dollar bills. And he'd appreciate it if they were consecutively numbered and un-circulated."

He said, "Art, *all* ten thousand dollar bills are uncirculated." [laughter] Finally he says, "OK. I don't like it, but I'll send them to you."

Joe Brown had his million dollars on display at the Horseshoe for a long time. When Benny Binion got out of jail he bought the club back, but the million in ten thousand dollar bills stayed there. A couple of years went by, and Benny called me one morning and asked if he could see me at one o'clock that afternoon. I said sure, and when I came back from lunch that day he was waiting for me in the lobby. I says, "You're early."

"Yeah," he says. "I want to get this over with." He walks into my office, and he pulls off one of his cowboy boots and turns it upside down and dumps sixty ten thousand dollar bills on my desk. Then he puts his boot back on, pulls the other one off and dumps out forty more. A million bucks in his boots! He said that Joe Brown had died, and he wanted me to send the money to Brown's widow. I was to get ahold of a banker in new Orleans who knew all about it and would take care of it.

I says, "Benny, how long were you sitting out there in the lobby?"

"Oh, five minutes."

The headquarters of Bank of Nevada was on the corner of First and Carson Streets then, and the Horseshoe was on the corner of Second and Fremont, which was two blocks away. I said, "You come over here alone?"

"Yep."

I said, "Jesus, isn't that taking a chance?"

"Well, I don't know. I got here, didn't I?" [laughter] He said, "About noon we got a bunch of security guards together and made a commotion there in the club. We had guys everywhere, and we took the big display panel into my office and locked the doors and took all the bills out, and I put them into my boots. We sat there until about a quarter till one, and then I sent out two guys carrying briefcases, each of them escorted by a couple of security guards. They went out the front door and headed toward the First National Bank on Third Street." He says, "I waited a minute, went out and looked around the casino, and then walked out the back door and down the alley and came over here."

I says, "Nobody guarding you?"

"Nope. Nobody with me."

I says, "Whooh, that's pretty dangerous isn't it?"

He puts his hand in his right front pocket and pulls out a little two-shot derringer: "I got this."

I said, "You could of got killed, Benny."

Benny said, "What difference does that make?" [laughter] And that was the end of it. Benny was really a character. I don't know what he'd done to go to prison, but he did a lot of good for the city of Las Vegas, and his family continues to.

# Part Three

*Running the Biggest Bank in Nevada:
Reno, 1967-1984*

# 17

## CEO of FNB

IN 1967 LAS VEGAS was just starting to get going. It was really the place to be. I had my own little show there with the Bank of Nevada, and it was great—I had everything I could want. Then the president of Western Bancorp, Clifford Tweter, called to ask if I would like to move up to Reno to become the next president of First National Bank of Nevada. I said no. Why leave the good thing that I had and go through all the turmoil of relocating my family to Reno just to get into a situation that I might fail at?

A couple of weeks went by and I got a phone call early one morning from Frank King, the chairman of Western Bancorp. He wanted me to fly down to Los Angeles to meet with him. We went over to the California Club for lunch, and after a lot of small talk he looked me in the eye and said, "Art, why don't you do me a favor? Why don't you just agree to move to Reno before I have to order you to do it?" That's when I knew

I was going to Reno. [laughter] "OK," I said, "that's what we'll do."

The First National Bank of Nevada had been started in Reno by a mule skinner in the early 1900s. Originally it was called the Farmers and Merchants Bank. Shortly after it was started, Governor Kirman and a fellow named Walter Harris bought it. When the bank crash came in the 1930s and President Roosevelt ordered all the banks closed, the First National locked its front door and put up a sign that said, "Closed by Presidential Decree." But word got out that if you went to the back door you could just walk in and do your business as usual.

The bank was real conservative and a very solvent bank for the time. Shortly after the bank holiday it was bought by Transamerica, and Carl Wente was sent over to run it. After five or six years he returned to Transamerica's San Francisco headquarters, and W. W. Hopper became the president. Bill Hopper was highly respected, but he was also . . . can you be too proper? Maybe he was too proper. He was extremely conservative, very dignified, a guy who could never let his hair down—to him, everything was just dead serious, and he lived the role of the stereotypical banker of his time: "Don't bother me with frivolous things, and don't talk about things that aren't real important." He was so *careful* about everything. I remember visiting him in his office once when I was still with Bank of Nevada: He sat behind his big desk, and when he got up to go over to the window while we were talking, he pulled out a key and locked his desk. [laughter] But he was a good banker, and he ran the bank until he retired as chairman of the board in 1958.

In the late 1930s a local guy named Eddie Questa had gone to work at the bank. He was Italian and he became friendly with old A. P. Giannini, who was head of Transamerica. Giannini took him over to the Bank of America, and Bank of America sent him to the Far East. Eddie was stationed in the Philippines and Bangkok and all over. When Bill Hopper came to the point in his life when he was ready to step down as president, Transamerica brought Eddie back to the bank where he had started and made him its president and chief executive officer.

Eddie and Bill had totally different personalties. Whereas Bill Hopper was conservative and careful almost to a fault, Eddie was aggressive and energetic and creative; and in my opinion, if Eddie had been president instead of Hopper in that period from 1937 to 1952, the bank would have grown a hell of a lot faster than it did, and Reno would have grown faster as a consequence. But who knows? Maybe Hopper's leadership was right for the time—the bank was just a little bank when he came up, but it grew to two hundred million dollars. The question is how much it would have grown if he hadn't been so conservative. Maybe it would've grown like hell and then gone broke! [laughter]

Eddie Questa was a bachelor; never got married. He had spent a long time in Bangkok, and when he built his house in Reno he brought a Siamese family over to be his housekeepers. Since he was single, had no kids, Eddie didn't need a lot, and whenever the bank would go to increase his salary, he'd say, "Whatever you want to give me, we'll just defer it to when I retire." Since he wasn't taking significant salary increases, the top guys under him wouldn't get much either—they couldn't be making more than the chairman. The raises they got were almost punitive, they were so small. After Harold Gorman retired we talked about it, and he said it had been terrible: for years they couldn't get any increases because Eddie didn't want one. And when Questa died and Gorman took over, he didn't go down to the holding company and say, "Look, I think I'm underpaid." He probably thought they'd say, "Then you're fired!" [laughter]

Bill Hopper continued as chairman of the board when Eddie became president in 1952, but there was no question who was running the bank—Eddie was! As chairman, Hopper ran the board meetings and that's all. For ten years Eddie did a great job. Then, tragically, in 1962 he was killed in the crash of an airplane piloted by his friend Newt Crumley down around Tonopah. Eddie's death caught the bank unprepared—there was a period there when they really didn't know where they wanted to go. They didn't have a guy in place; the succession was out of whack. At Eddie's funeral, standing in the rain up at the cemetery, I was approached by Maury Stans, the president of the holding company. He said, "We don't know what we're going to do about Questa's successor. We're considering two or three names. Would you like to be one of the candidates?" I was happy where I was; I didn't have any interest in moving to Reno, and I said no. They picked Harold Gorman to become president of the bank, and they brought Bill Hopper out of retirement to be chairman of the board, and that told the story. It was never said, but they weren't really sure that Harold was the guy, so they brought back Hopper, who was predictable. He had a track record and they knew where he was coming from.

Harold Gorman was perhaps even more conservative than Hopper—so conservative that in his eagerness to do nothing wrong he may have constricted the bank, held back its growth. Harold was born in Carlin, Nevada, grew up in Nevada, worked in the bank all his life, and he never bought a house! He always thought the prices would come down. [laughter] To the day he died, he and his wife lived in an apartment. He was awfully conservative.

In 1964 Bill Hopper resigned as chairman of the board, and Harold Gorman moved from the presidency to the board chairmanship. E. H. Fitz, Bert Fitz, became the president. Bert had come over from Bank of America in the late 1940s to become First National's cashier. When he became president, he was just president; he wasn't chief operating officer. Bert was another extremely conservative guy—very bright, very good, but limited because he came from the operations side of the bank, where the pick and shovel guys are. (The romantic side of banking is the lending side.)

Bert Fitz had the title of president, and he was a steadying influence who kept the operating side of the bank in good shape, but he was really not what a president normally would be. Gorman was actually running things. So when you talk about past presidents, you can almost pull Bert Fitz out of there and say, "Well, he was the operating guy." What you really had was Questa and Hopper and Gorman running the bank from 1952 to 1968.

When Harold Gorman approached sixty-five, Western Bancorp started looking for someone to take his place, and that's when they decided I should move to Reno. In order to accommodate that, Bert Fitz retired as president in 1967, and I came up as president and chief executive officer. Harold was still chairman, but when he retired the following year I became chairman of the board as well. And that's how I became president and chairman of the board of First National Bank of Nevada.

Of course, before I agreed to take the job I talked things over with my family. I was probably more apprehensive than any of them. Charlotte's always been, "Whatever's good for you, Dad, is good for all of us," and she was fully supportive. The kids didn't care; they said, "Dad, just don't make us move in the middle of a semester." So I got a little apartment in Reno and commuted for a couple of months until the kids' school terms ended, and then everybody moved up to Reno in January of 1968. We enrolled Debbie in Manogue, Reno's Catholic high school, and Matt and Blake went into public schools. Barbara had just started her first year at the University of Santa Clara.

As soon as I accepted the job, Fred Huber, the holding company's vice president, went to Reno to tell Gorman and Fitz what was going to happen. Breaking the news was a real tough thing because nobody at FNB in Reno ever thought someone from Las Vegas would be brought in to take over.

I was to be president and chief executive officer, and I asked Huber, "What kind of a raise do I get?"

He said, "You don't get a raise."

I said, "Wait a minute!"

He said, "We'll talk to you about it next May."

It turned out that I was already earning the same salary at the little Bank of Nevada that Harold Gorman got for running the First National Bank. They said, "We can't bring you up and pay you more than the chairman." The company took care of my salary as soon as Gorman retired.


One of the reasons Frank King wanted me to go to Reno was that Western Bancorporation owned two banks in Nevada. He said, "We don't need two administrations; it isn't cost effective. So when you get to Reno, I want you to engineer a merger of the Bank of Nevada into the First National Bank."

Soon after I got to Reno I got started on the merger, but the Justice Department said we couldn't do it. They said Western Bancorp would have 87 percent of the business in Nevada if the two banks merged, and that was in violation of anti-trust laws. We said, "So? We've got 87 percent with them not merged." [laughter] They weren't persuaded, so we got the best law firm in Washington, D.C., working on it. One of the lawyers would fly out to Reno every few months to brief me on what was going on. One day he called and said, "Art, how long would it take you to merge those banks?"

I said, "Three months."

He said, "Do it. It *will* be approved."

To this day I don't know how they pulled it off. We never called on our congressmen to intervene, and we didn't pull any other strings that I was aware of—the Justice Department just changed its mind. So we got our banks merged.

Although First National Bank of Nevada publicized that they were statewide, they hadn't done much in Las Vegas while I was at Bank of Nevada. In fact, for a long time they had acted like they didn't want to admit that there *was* a Las Vegas, and when they made me their president I thought I was going to a bank that wasn't very progressive, based on its performance in Vegas.

Once I got to Reno it didn't take me long to realize that I'd underestimated the organization. At least it had no problems with bad loans or bad operations. It was one of the best in the country when looked at from that standpoint, but it just wasn't progressive—it seemed to me that it was really just interested in maintaining the status quo. For example, the loan policy: All banks are restricted as to what types of loans they can make and the amounts they can advance against certain types of collateral. FNB was so conservative that they were more restrictive than the law required. When they made real estate loans, where the law said you could go 80 percent of appraisal, they would only go 60 percent, which amounted to a penalty to the borrower.

The bank may have been conservative, but I had inherited a gold mine of talent and other resources. I'd just say, "What about this?" And they'd come back in the afternoon and say, "It's done." It was such a revelation! Not to belittle the Bank of Nevada—the Bank of Nevada was a wonderful experience for me—but it was like I'd been driving a pickup truck and now the guy says, "Here, drive this sports car." First National Bank had the money and the horsepower and the people to do things that would have been unimaginable at Bank of Nevada. I mean, we even had branch managers with twenty years experience. We had Lino del Grande, Carl Friesen; we had Bill Boman out in Fallon, and we had a guy named Bill Elwell, who had been at Yerington forever and knew more about farm loans than any guy in the system. Roland Mudge had been at Winnemucca for years, and before him was a guy named Al Risso, who also had worked over in the Sparks branch. (Risso had married Virginia Cross, who was my second grade school teacher.)

Ernie Martinelli was the bank's cashier and Joe Sbragia was our senior credit officer. (Joe was the man who had hired me when I went to work for the bank down in Sparks in 1942.) We had Jordan Crouch

135

(everyone remembers Jordan Crouch—he never stopped talking, but the people loved him); and we had guys like Cecil Clark, who had been the branch manager downstairs forever and ever. Hank Gallues, a little Basque guy who was just a terrific banker, was a credit officer, and Buzzy Allen (L. S. Allen, who later became the executive vice president of Bank of America in Reno) was head of operations for our bank. Buzzy was probably the finest bank operations guy I've ever been around. He could sit there and look like he was doing nothing, and he'd have four balls in the air and everything going at once. He was absolutely amazing; a wonderful fellow.

The bank had such talented people that you didn't have to start them up—you just opened the gate and here they came. The old attitude had been that if customers came in the door wanting a loan, we'd listen to them. Now we had Ernie Martinelli *hauling* them through the door. [laughter] And Hank Gallues is sitting there sorting them out like they're sheep, saying, "That's bad; kick it out and keep this." They were quite a combination. It was almost unbelievable, the stuff that was coming in, and we were just cherry picking it. That attitude caught on in a hurry, and man, the young aggressive guys ate it up: "Here we go!" And I think the oldtimers kind of enjoyed watching it. The bank grew almost twenty percent in my first year as president.[1] It

[1] In 1968 net operating earnings went up 21 percent, deposits and loans rose by 18 percent, and the bank's total resources rose to almost five hundred and forty million dollars.

was an experience that we'll never have again, because banking will never again be like it was in those days.

Once we realized what we had, it was just a matter of finding out how you do this and do that, and that led to an understanding that if we were to continue to grow, it couldn't be with the existing setup. We were going to need more branches, more branch managers, and more and more people. And we couldn't continue under the old system where every branch manager in the state had a lending limit which he couldn't exceed without the approval of Joe Sbragia in Reno. There weren't enough Joe Sbragias to go around. [laughter] So in 1968 I decided to break our operations in the state up into geographical regions. Initially there was some resistance to the idea (it's the same old story—everybody resists change), but I was able to overcome it and put the plan into effect.

We set up three different regions, each under a newly created regional vice presidency. Everything from Tonopah south went into the southern region; the bulk of our branches at that time were in Washoe County and Douglas County, and we called that our northern region; and everything from Fallon to the Utah border went into the eastern region. The eastern region was made up basically of cow county banks, which were a completely different breed than the First and Virginia branch. We put Bill Elwell in charge of that region because he was experienced and understood what went on in rural communities. Harry Fletcher had been managing our main branch in Las Vegas for years, and we put him in charge of the southern region. James H. Bradshaw, Bud Bradshaw, was named regional vice president to handle the northern branches. They all reported to our new overall executive vice president, Henry Gallues.

Bill Elwell, Bud Bradshaw and Harry Fletcher really made the bank run. Each had a marketing guy and a loan guy under him, and each had his own lending limit for his unit. In turn they assigned limits out to their branch managers. It was like a pyramid with Gallues at the top. If one of the regional vice presidents got a loan that took him over his lending limit, he would go to Gallues, who had a limit big enough to cover most loans from the regions. The really big loan applications ended up in the Finance Committee chaired by Joe Sbragia. And the marketing guys would take support from Jordan Crouch.

It took a little while to get this system developed, but here's how well it ran: Hank Gallues was an Air Force pilot in Korea, and he stayed in the Air National Guard. Just after we got this system organized and running, Hank got called up for service in Viet Nam. So now the guy who's the head of our operating pyramid is gone. Bud Bradshaw called me up and said, "Art, I know you got a problem there. If it will help I'll take his job, and I'll step down the minute he walks back in the bank." That's the kind of loyalty we had there. Bud was a very capable guy, and he became the executive V. P. until Hank came back.

In addition to reorganizing our operations, I began putting an emphasis on training and recruitment. We had a great group in place, but I knew that the experienced guys who were making things work were not going to be there forever. We needed to find and develop their replacements. We interviewed on campuses like some of the big companies, and I asked the University of Nevada to give me three good students every year out of the business school, and I'd try to put them on. We also ran our own training within the bank. If we decided that someone was a candidate to become an officer and get onto the official staff, we'd put him in a training program. If he was going to go to the operating side he'd do everything there was in a branch. He'd be a teller; he'd be a clerk—they went through the whole gamut so they knew everything that went on in the operating side of the bank. If they were going to be a branch manager or going to the lending side, we'd put them through a credit training program.

In the 1970s FNB of Nevada became one of the most successful banks in the Western Bancorp chain. When you talk about how a bank performs, you look at how much money it makes for every hundred dollars in deposits. We were making a dollar eighty-five! Now, you can understand that a big unit bank might make that much (probably won't, but might), but we were a branch system making a buck eighty-five on every hundred dollars of deposits. That's after taxes, everything. That's the bottom line, and it was unheard of. Normally if you get to a dollar you're really hitting home runs, and we're making a dollar eighty-five. (Even when I came to Reno in 1968, FNB was probably making about a dollar twenty-five, a dollar thirty on a hundred. This bank's always been a cash cow.)

Several things contributed to our success: Nevada was growing like crazy; we were the biggest bank in the state, which gave us lots of leverage (everyone wants to be with the big fellow); we operated in an area in which the cost of banking was much lower than in certain areas of California; and we had the best people working for us. All these guys needed was motivation, and I think that all my life I've been a motivator—I like to be a doer, but I think I motivate better than I do. I was always saying, "What can we do better? Let's not react to situations; let's create situations," and I think we did a pretty good job of that. By the time I retired, we had sixty-five branches and three billion dollars in deposits. It was fun!

Western Bancorp owned a total of twenty-three banks scattered throughout the West. All of us had different names, and we got to thinking, "This is kind of goofy. Why don't we get a name that recognizes that we're all part of the same system?" I was on the executive committee at the time, and we had meeting after meeting trying to come up with a name that said, "If you bank with us, you bank with other states all over the West." Finally Ken Kauffman, the corporation's legal counsel, came up with the idea of calling us First Interstate Banks. There was a big debate over that: can

140

we really afford to be a First Interstate Bank if that makes us a FIB? [laughter]

In 1981 FNB became First Interstate Bank of Nevada. Nothing changed except our name, but we made a big deal of it. We had all new signs up, and they were draped, and everyone went out in front of the branch and I yanked the cord and we became First Interstate Bank.

# 18

*Bill Harrah's Banker*

BILL HARRAH STARTED IN RENO with a little bingo parlor in the 1930s. In those days Pappy Smith owned and operated the town—nobody started a casino unless he said it was OK. Well, Pappy didn't care about bingo, didn't want it in his casino (Harold's Club), so he lets this guy Harrah start a bingo joint, and the next thing he knows Harrah's is bigger than Harold's.

First National Bank was Bill Harrah's bank, and soon after I became president he got in touch with me through Maurice Sheppard. We got to know each other, and I discovered that Bill was almost a recluse. He was a hard guy to be around. For years we'd have lunch once a month, and I would go with him one time and he'd go with me the next. He would usually take me to his private dining room, a little room at the rear of Harrah's Steak House. He'd come in the back way and we'd have lunch, and then he'd leave and go up the stairway and across the alley and into his office and never see a soul other than his waiter and me. The public didn't even know that room was there.

The next month I'd take him someplace. But where do you take Bill Harrah for lunch? And wherever you go, he's got a bodyguard that has to go with you. What do you do with the bodyguard? I'd take Bill out to the Hidden Valley Country Club and tell them I wanted a table over in the corner; or I'd take him down to Anderson's, the dimly-lit steak place in Park Lane. The toughest part of all was having lunch, because all he'd do was sit and look at you. [laughter] Very seldom would he say anything. Very quiet.

Bill was really a strange guy. One time he was going some place and he stopped in Stanley, Idaho, overnight, and he fell in love with the joint. Most people just stopped for gas there, but he ended up buying the town before he was finished. He decided to buy the local airport, and he thought he had, but he discovered that the last two thousand feet of runway was on Forest Service land or something, and he almost had a stroke over that. [laughter]

And the money Bill spent on building his Middle Fork Lodge! It was a beautiful lodge with cabins and swimming pools and some huge hot springs, right on the Middle Fork of the Salmon River in Idaho. In the little bar there I remember seeing a picture of this fellow who flew a Twin Otter from Challis, Idaho, to the Middle Fork, fourteen hundred trips in one year, hauling material to build that lodge. And if they needed a Caterpillar or something like that in there, they just walked it right up the river. There were no roads; they just drove it up the river until they got it where they wanted it.

The lodge was a fantastic place. It was supposedly to entertain Harrah's corporate guests, and a few went up there. But when Bill was there, he generally was alone with his family or maybe with a close friend, and he lived in the main lodge and you lived somewhere else. He had a full crew of wranglers and workers up there. They cut hay and they had lots of horses and they'd take you fishing or they'd take you elk hunting on horseback; take you deer hunting. That was his style.

For all his eccentricities, Bill Harrah had a good balance sheet and he was making money. It was impossible to think that he wouldn't continue to be successful. The only thing the bank ever questioned was the amount of the company's money he was putting into his auto collection. His love wasn't the casinos—the casinos were just a means to an end, which for him was that collection.[1] He had an office down there which was every bit as nice as his office at Harrah's headquarters, and he spent a lot of time in it.

Bill loved to drive fast . . . very fast. In the old days Nevada didn't have a speed limit on rural roads, and

---

[1] At the time of Bill Harrah's death, the Harrah's Auto Collection numbered 1,400 antique and vintage automobiles in various stages of restoration. The collection, with associated garages, offices and library, filled three warehouses on Glendale avenue in Sparks, just east of Reno.

when he got out there to Washoe Valley it was just "Katy, bar the door!" One day he says, "Come along with me; I'm going up to Tahoe." He's driving one of his Ferraris, and as we drop down over that little hill at Washoe Lake he says, "You want to know how fast this car will go?"

"No."

He got on that straight stretch, and it just started humming, and I sat back in my seat and closed my eyes and thought, "Jesus, will I be glad when we get to the end of this valley."

And he said, "You want to know how fast we're going?"

"No."

He said, "We're doing a hundred and seventy-six."

He loved speed and he loved the Indianapolis 500. He took me and my wife twice. It was a spectacle I will never forget. When we landed in Indianapolis there would be a car waiting for us with a driver, and Bill and I and our wives would get in, and there would be six motorcycle policemen to escort us down to our hotel. Now, you can't imagine the traffic that's in Indianapolis during the week of the 500. It's gridlocked . . . but not for Bill Harrah. The motorcycle police turn on their sirens and red lights, and we go right to the hotel, and Bill gets out and everything he wants is there.

When we go to dinner that night, it's the same thing; and when we go to the races, we don't get up and start for the track at daylight along with the other half million spectators—Bill Harrah gets up at his usual time, and

146

the motorcycle police bring us to the track a half hour before the race begins. And where do we sit? Up in about the fifth row of the balcony right above the finish line. Perfect seats. That's what Bill loved. Then his big deal was that the minute the race was over he had to be the first guy to his airplane and the first plane off the runway going home; so the police would meet us in the hall and escort us again. It was almost unreal. In fact, it got embarrassing. Every time you'd hear a siren or see a policeman you'd say, "Here comes Bill Harrah." [laughter]

When I arrived in Reno Maurice Sheppard was president of Harrah's, Lloyd Dyer was the executive vice president, and Rome Andreotti was the guy who knew gaming and ran the casinos. (Rome was very capable—a strong, two-fisted, no bullshit guy.) They were running the place, but Bill was truly the boss. He owned Harrah's 100 percent; he had no partners, and he did as he pleased. When his people talked about stock options or retirement pensions, he'd say, "Look, I'll pay you guys better than anyone else in the industry, but you can worry about your own retirement. I'm not going to give you both." Kind of contrary to what business was doing in those days, but that was Bill's idea.

If I remember correctly, when Bill first took the company public in 1971 he kept 80 percent of its stock. I went on his board of directors, and I could tell that he had a real problem handling the concept of partners— why did he have to care about what the guys who owned

20 percent thought? "It's still my company; I own 80 percent of it." You'd go to a board meeting and it wouldn't last ten minutes. Sometimes there'd be only one item on the agenda, and everybody'd say, "Aye," and Bill would say "We're adjourned," and he'd get up and leave.

Bill didn't feel comfortable outside of his own group, so on a board of seven or eight people he had only two outside directors, Mead Dixon and myself. (And I was Bill's banker, and Mead was his attorney.) With Mead Dixon, spades were spades and hearts were hearts, and he wouldn't call you a heart if you were a spade. We had had kind of a bumpy introduction. After I'd been president of FNB four or five months I was having dinner at the Steak House one night with Wallie Warren, and Wallie said, "That's Mead Dixon over there. I'd like you to meet him." So I went over and he introduced me.

Mead looked at me and said, "Art Smith, huh? You the new guy at the bank?"

I said, "Yeah."

"Well," he said, "Harrah's has had an application at your bank for a construction loan for six months, and we haven't heard a damn thing. I guess we're going to have start over."

I said, "Oh, that won't be necessary." And that was the end of our introduction.

The next day at the bank I said, "What's holding up this thing with Harrah's?"

"Oh, we're busy."

I said, "Busy, my ass! We're going to find out what's going on and we're going to give Harrah's an answer today." We got ahold of an insurance company down in Galveston, Texas, and they agreed to take the loan, and I called up Bill Harrah two days later and said, "Mr. Harrah, your loan's been approved." Then when Harrah wanted to build his other tower I got our sister bank in California to help us out, and between the two of us we put the whole thing together for him.

Bill Harrah's emphasis on quality was ultimately the source of his success, even though he wasn't much of a hands-on manager. He might have been in the old days, but when I knew him he had all these guys around that did everything for him. He'd say, "You take care of it, Shep," or Rome, or Lloyd.

He was such a stickler! Our bank's old Second and Virginia branch was right next to his casino, and our sidewalk was grimy and we couldn't get it clean. So he said, "Do you mind if I clean it?" He had his guys out there with scrubbers, and they cleaned it, but it wasn't good enough for him. Finally he called me up one day and said, "Art, I want to replace that damned sidewalk if you'll let me."

I said, "Do you realize that the basement of the bank stretches out underneath the sidewalk? When you lift that sidewalk up you're going to open up the basement. It will cost you a fortune."

He said, "I don't care what it costs," and he went ahead and did it.

Bill was an absolute perfectionist, and he had to have the best hotel-casino in the business. Touring Europe he stayed in hotel rooms that had little bars, drink cabinets, and he came back and said, "Now, look, we got to do it this way." And when he built the hotel at Lake Tahoe every room had to have two bathrooms, a "his" and a "hers," with telephones and little five-inch televisions in both. We were looking at the plans in a board meeting, and I said, "Jesus, Bill, do you have any idea what it costs to put in two bathrooms?"

He said, "No."

I said, "Why would you ever want to put two bathrooms in a regular hotel room?"

He looked at me and said, "Because I've always wanted to own a hotel that had two bathrooms in every room." That ended the conversation. And that was it. [laughter]

Bill treated himself and his family well. He would take the company's G-2, which was the finest corporate type aircraft in the world in those days, and send it over to Italy to pick up one of his sons; or he'd use it to fly up to the Mayo Clinic for a physical examination. Finally Mead and I said, "We can't handle this. He's using that plane for personal use and he's going to have to pay for it." We handed him a bill one day, and it was a big number—over three hundred thousand dollars. Mead told him, "Bill, you can't use the company plane for personal business. If you want to, you must pay just what you'd pay if you rented it." Poor old Bill almost had a stroke, but he paid it.

150

Bill would go back east to the Mayo Clinic regularly. He was a stickler for having his health checked and having his people get physicals—even us board members. When I was on the board I was told that the company would be tickled to have me go to Mayo's once a year for a physical, and the company would pay for it. They didn't say you had to, but the last sentence was, "You know, Mr. Harrah really believes in that." So when it came time for Shep or someone to go back I'd say, "OK, I'll go with you." We'd take the company airplane.

Well, in 1978, on one of Bill's visits to the clinic they discovered an aneurysm on his renal artery. He was sitting on a time bomb. They decided that they'd go in and do some preventive surgery, and they picked a date, and he went back for it, and the next thing I know Mead Dixon is calling me. He said, "Art, Bill's had a lot of blood transfusions, and he's all wired up on life support machines, and he's the color of a beet." Bill's wife, Verna, was there. She was worried to death. Mead later told me that the doctors let him know that Bill wasn't going to make it, so Mead told Verna to go on back to the hotel room—that he would stay at the hospital and keep her posted. As soon as she left, they took off the life supports and Bill Harrah passed away.

Following Bill Harrah's death Mead Dixon became chairman of the board. Mead had one of the best minds that I was ever around in my whole life. I mean, it was a steel trap. He could be the most pleasant guy in the world, or he could be the most obnoxious, but all the

151

time he was thinking. To me, he was brilliant. It was easy to say, "Hey, I agree with you Mead. I think you're on the right track and I'll support you."

Mead wanted to sell Harrah's to Holiday Inns. Kemmons Wilson, who started Holiday Inns and whom I'd known for quite a while, used to call me all the time and say, "We want to buy Harrah's, and I want to come out and talk to Bill Harrah about it." After Bill's death, when they got real serious, Holiday Inns brought their whole board out to look at the properties. Harrah's had a big dinner for them at Villa Harrah, Bill's place up at the lake. The thing that might have clinched the deal was when one of their guys who worked for the Illinois Institute of Technology came over to me and said, "Just tell me, what do you really think?"

I said, "Well, you've seen it all. It's true that maybe the company could be more efficient, have better earnings, but the one thing you may not have thought about is that car collection." It was on the balance sheet for something like twelve or fourteen million bucks, "but," I said, "the thing is probably worth seventy or eighty million if you want to sell it a car at a time." And boy, his eyebrows shot up and he looked around. That car collection may have been what finally cinched the deal—assets that didn't show on the balance sheet.

In 1980 the company was purchased by Holiday Inns, which dissolved Harrah's board. Harrah's was run better than Holiday at the time—no question that from a quality standpoint it was the better of the two. It didn't have the horsepower that Holiday brought to the table, but it had the knowhow and the quality and the reputation. As part of the purchase deal, Mead insisted that he had to go on Holiday's board and bring one other person with him. He named me.

While I was on the board I had to be licensed in New Jersey, because Harrah's and Holiday were expanding into New Jersey. What I went through wasn't a licensing procedure, it was an inquisition! [laughter] I sent in an application that went on for pages and pages, and one of the questions was, "Do you own a gun?"

"Yes, I own many guns."

"List the types and serial numbers."

I wrote down the information they wanted, but I also lined up all my guns in my den and took a picture of them with my Polaroid, and I put it on the application.

When the New Jersey gaming agent came out to interview me he said, "Let me see your check book."

I said, "I got three check books."

He said, "Bring me all three of them."

He goes through them, and here's a check to this, and one to that, and here's one for cash—three hundred dollars. He said, "Now, what did you do with that cash?"

I said, "You aren't going to believe this."

"What am I not going to believe?"

I said, "I don't remember what I did with it." [laughter]

He said, "You know, one of the agents back in New Jersey wants to know if you're a revolutionary."

I said, "What makes you think I'm a revolutionary?"

He said, "All them guns! They saw the picture."

The president of a bank, a revolutionary? But that was their mentality.

# 19

---

## *Credit Cards, Credit Companies*

THERE WAS SOME GOOD and some bad about the introduction of credit cards. A credit card was good for the
guy who could use one and manage it and take care of it
carefully, but I'm told that when credit cards first came
out, over 50 percent of all consumer buying was impulse
buying. If you've got a credit card in your pocket and
you're an impulse buyer, it might not be good for you.
You go home and you think, "Why did I buy that? I
bought it because I had a credit card."

Bank of America started the whole credit card thing
back in the 1960s with their Bank Americard. When the
Bank Americard caught on they got going so good that
they started franchising banks throughout the country.
Then banks on the west coast got to thinking, "Wait a
minute. This bank is sitting right in our front yard in
San Francisco issuing all these cards, but they aren't
going to give us a card because we're competitors? Well,
screw them! We'll start our own credit card program."

They created Western States Bank Card Association, which developed the Master Charge program. A man named Bill Elmer from Wells Fargo Bank led the organization.

When I became president of FNB, we had no credit card, and our board was absolutely adamant that we should never issue one. They said, "We don't want that; we shouldn't have it; it's bad." They may have been right. [laughter] If you managed it wrong you got in trouble, and most banks did have some problems with it in the early days.

Late in 1967 we were approached to join Western States and get into their Master Charge program, but Gorman was negative and so was I. We said, "The credit card thing is just a fad, and it's going to go away. We won't get involved in it." Then I got a call from our holding company, Western Bancorp. They said, "We understand that you don't want to have a credit card. Do you know anything about them?"

"Well, not too much."

"Would you object if we sent some people to Reno to show you what you could do with the card? It would be a complete study of the good, the bad, the cost, the returns. We'll pay for it."

I thought, "It's free; we might find out something good." A big west coast consulting firm came to Reno and took a look at our customer base and at the demographics of Nevada, and came up with a report that was pretty glowing. So we said, "We were wrong. Yeah, we'd like to join the Master Charge program." By early 1968 we were in.

Reluctant though we had been, once FNB decided to issue a credit card we just promoted the hell out of it. (Martinelli and Gallues were out there promoting it, and we made up little plaques for merchants that said, "We honor Master Charge." We even had me up on a step ladder hanging a Master Charge sign on a service station.) But we were very careful about how we issued our cards. Some banks just had wholesale mailings, but we were more conservative than the rest—we put almost every applicant through a credit check. Even that wasn't enough. You issue a card that's good for twelve hundred bucks, and if the holder runs it up tomorrow, you got to collect. Well, we had horrendous losses. When I retired in 1984 we were writing off three hundred thousand a month on those cards. Factoring in the income from them, we may not have been losing money, but our percentage of loss on the cards versus our percentage of loss on the other loans in the bank was ridiculous. And we were doing better than most banks.

Some banks just issued cards, but at FNB we were also a merchant bank. Here's how it works: You've got a credit card from our bank; we issued it to you. There are banks who do just that, and that's all—when their card is used they won't take the credit slip and redeem it. If you redeem the paper, now you become a merchant bank. In other words, if Menard's charged your card for a suit, they'd bring the credit slip to us to cash it. If we weren't a merchant bank they'd have had to take it to some other Master Charge or Visa bank to redeem it. So we went both sides, and that meant we had to deal with the issue of loss to counterfeit cards.

You could buy a counterfeit card for five hundred bucks. There was a time when guys just went down alleys in New York, behind the big restaurants, the Stork Club and Twenty-One, and pulled the transparents out of the trash and got the numbers off them. Once you get a number you don't care whose name's on it—you can emboss a card with that number. This creates a real accounting nightmare. Say a guy counterfeits some First Interstate Bank card, and you're a merchant, and you accept his card for a five hundred dollar TV. You bring the credit slip down to the bank and we say, "That's counterfeit." We hand it back to you. Now, who absorbs the loss? If the bank took the attitude, "Well, you're going to eat it, Mr. Merchant," you'd say, "I'll eat this one, but I'll never eat another one because I'll never accept a Master Card again." Instead, what happened was the bank would send the card over to the Western State Bank Card Association, and they'd pick up the loss. All the member banks were contributing into that fund, and some of the money we contributed may have been used to pick up a loss to some merchant in Salinas, California, from a guy who got a card from a bank in Odgen, Utah. We covered losses that way, and that got to be a big number.

Bank of America decided to change the name of its card to make it more marketable around the world. They had a big contest to find a name (anything to get publicity) and "Visa" won out. FNB later added Visa, because certain businesses weren't Master Charge merchants and some people didn't want to carry a Master Charge card. (There's actually very little difference between the two. It's like K-Mart and Wal-Mart—you go in and buy the same thing, but they got different names on the stores. Just about what it is.)

Later on a consortium of eastern banks decided they wanted to put together a card to be a national competitor to Visa. They came to Western States Bank Card Association to see if they could acquire our Master Charge program. Bill Elmer said, "Well, yeah; but we're going to set some standards for the card, and we're going to insist that we get two seats on the board of directors that runs this." They agreed to that, but they changed the card's name to Master Card.

Eventually I became president of Western States, and later I went on the Master Card International board too. We were Master Card for the world. We met four times a year, and one meeting was always in another country. I got to travel to Japan, to Rome, to Australia, Madrid, London, Stockholm, Zurich . . . you name it. I got to meet some interesting guys and learn a little about how banks operate in the rest of the world.

Sometime in the early 1970s I got an idea: big credit companies would have an advantage if they moved their headquarters to Nevada because Nevada had no corporate income tax. We began looking for a captive operation, one that was wholly owned by a parent company. That way we wouldn't have to deal with a bunch of people to get the thing moved; the head of the company can say we're going or we're not. Deere & Company of Moline, Illinois, had a credit company to finance buyers of John Deere equipment—big ticket items like harvesters, big plows, tractors, backhoes, scrapers, and so forth. They were paying Illinois state income tax on the interest. I suggested that they move that operation to Nevada and we would rent them an office in the bank. I contacted a fellow named Cliff Peterson, who was the senior vice president and head of the financial department. He sent some guys out to investigate the situation, and pretty soon he told us, "We're going to do it."

When we brought Deere Credit to Reno they came with a billion dollars worth of paper, and I think our bank was about an eight hundred million dollar bank. So they were bigger than the bank, but they were operating out of one room with a staff of just four people. [laughter] Their office, which was on the seventh or eighth floor of our First and Virginia building, wasn't even as big as my living room. When they were ready to occupy it we took the windows out, got a big crane, picked up their fireproof safes and swung them in. They actually domiciled the notes right in Reno, and the payments came here and the interest was collected here.

160

Deere & Company owned captive insurance companies, too, which they moved here. Being located in Reno saved the company millions and millions of dollars, and I wound up on their board because of that. First I was invited to join their Tahoe Insurance Company board; then they put me on the Sierra General Insurance board; and then they formed the John Deere Insurance Group, and they put me on that board.

I hate to tell you the amount of money that Deere has made over the years they have been in Reno, and their business license fees have put a lot into the city treasury. But when Nevada was considering a 10 percent corporate business tax in 1994, John Deere Credit already had a site picked out in another state. They were leaving the day that bill passed. They were going to bail out. It didn't happen; but if it does, they're gone, and they'll go right to South Dakota.

# 20

## *The Red Line and Downtown Development*

POP SOUTHWORTH, George Southworth, was one of the most powerful guys in Reno in the old days. He owned a tobacco store on Virginia Street almost where the Fitzgerald Hotel is now; and it was said that Raymond I. Smith, the fellow who owned Harold's Club, sponsored him and that they worked together politically. Pop Southworth was responsible for getting a "red line" started, forbidding further expansion of unrestricted gaming outside the downtown core of Reno. I heard that the people who had the existing gaming downtown, principally Harold's Club, wanted to keep gambling within an area where they could exert some control. Southworth was on the city council and he was briefly the mayor of Reno in the late 1940s, and apparently he was able to get that ordinance put in. I have also been told that the red line was expanded and changed several times, but that it seemed always to be something that benefitted the big gaming interests in downtown Reno.

Oddly enough, the only places that had gaming *and* rooms were outside the red line. The Mapes Hotel had rooms, and the Riverside, and the Holiday Inn on the river. And by 1970 Reno suffered from a serious shortage of hotel rooms.

I'd been back in Reno about three years when I got a call from the mayor, Roy Bankofier, while I was on vacation in Hawaii. He said, "We want to put together a committee to look at how we license gaming in the city of Reno. It's kind of helter skelter now, and we really don't know what's right and what's wrong about it. Would you head up a committee that I'll pick? I want the committee to make recommendations for how our licensing ordinance should be worded." I agreed to do it, and the mayor put together a committee representative of all the non-gaming business interests in town.

We met for several months two or three times a week with people who were really important in Reno, and business people who wanted to see that the right thing was done. The committee was interested primarily in the expansion of unrestricted gaming outside the four-block core of the city, and the related issue of Reno's need for more hotel rooms. These were strictly business concerns; we weren't looking into the expansion of gaming to other areas of the community as a social issue. Twenty-five years ago we didn't have the type of thing that's going on downtown now—today the area around the casinos is pretty seedy, but back then you had operators who wouldn't let that happen; and you didn't have the social do-gooders then that you have now.

It was kind of a fun committee because we had all the horsepower in town in the way of business people, and we were under no pressure. The City Council wasn't pressuring us and the gaming industry wasn't pressuring us . . . well, one of the operators did ask us to delay our decision for a couple of weeks: Lincoln Fitzgerald had his club there between Harrah's and Harold's on Virginia Street, and it was a slaughter house—they just made money like you can't believe! About the time our committee was formed Lincoln was sitting on so much surplus cash that if he didn't do something with it he was going to get a huge tax bill. As the committee neared the finish of its work he called me one day and said, "Before you guys come down with a bunch of rules, there's something I want to do." He had decided to put up the building that is now Fitzgerald's Hotel-Casino. That would get rid of his excess cash, but he didn't know what we were going to do about expansion downtown, and he didn't want to get caught out. He asked me to delay the release of our report for two weeks so he could get his ducks on the pond before the council acted on our recommendations. I said, "I'm not sure we can do that, Lincoln," but in the end we recommended to the council that the ordinance not go into effect until ninety days after it had passed. That gave Lincoln Fitzgerald time to do what he had to do.

The committee unanimously agreed that the city's tourism economy needed more entertainment to attract additional visitors and more hotel rooms to increase convention business during the slower gaming months. We ultimately came up with a recommendation to the City Council, a five point program. Point one was to eliminate the red line—no geographic considerations should be involved in granting unlimited gaming licenses. (We'd have two types of licenses; a restricted license where you were limited to Keno, and an unrestricted license for full casinos.) However (and this was the most important point), in the future anyone who received an unlimited gaming license would have to construct a hotel with a minimum of one hundred rooms in addition to the casino. That was really what we were after.

Of course, with the rooms, most hotels also have a show room, and that brought the entertainment that we were also looking for. And our thinking went that if a guy builds rooms and restaurants in his hotel, we can have conventions there. As I recall, we didn't have a convention authority in 1970 and nobody was even talking about convention facilities. In this regard Reno once again was quite a bit behind Las Vegas in development. By 1970, Las Vegas had plenty of convention capacity. They had a number of very large hotels that were associated with casinos, and most of them had a huge dining room and a convention facility. And Reno had zero.

Before our committee made its recommendations, there had been practically no rooms downtown—the Mapes and the Riverside and the Holiday were all outside the redlined downtown core. Most of the casinos just had some sort of a deal with a motel or two where they would place their customers. Harold's Club owned its own motel, but it was two miles from the casino—the old Pony Express out at the Y in Sparks, where B Street breaks off from Prater Way. It was quite famous; everyone around the state knew the Pony Express Motel, and it was a money maker. It became part of Harold's advertising: "We'll put you up in the Pony Express."

Twenty-five years later almost every casino in town has rooms, but in those days the casinos considered themselves as being in the gambling business and only that. Fourth Street was lined with motels, and that was Fourth Street's business. It was just, "You do your thing and I'll do mine." Of course, it soon became obvious that there's really an upside to having rooms in your casino—Harrah's took off and became *the* casino operation in northern Nevada when they built their hotel. I think history will prove that if Reno hadn't gotten all those rooms it wouldn't have grown like it has.

At Bank of Nevada I had been used to operating under state laws and regulations that I thought I knew pretty well, but many of them didn't apply at the First National Bank. Our controller would come up to me and say, "Mr. Smith, you can't do that. This is a national bank." Even the rules concerning political donations were different than they were for Bank of Nevada. National banks can't make any donations, period—it's the law. When I was at the Bank of Nevada, if Bill Raggio or whoever came by and wanted a political donation, I could make it up to a certain level. Now the same guy comes in and I can't do it, and he says, "Wait a minute, Smith, are you pulling my leg? You did it before." But the laws are totally different—the bank can't get involved in politics. Sometimes you wish it could.

In 1979 Barbara Bennett was elected mayor of Reno on a platform that promised to restrain growth. She had a following, but I think she was in over her head. In fact I'm not sure that Barbara Bennett and her administration didn't hold the city back. In my opinion, when Roy Bankofier was mayor, and John Chism and Claude Hunter and Ernie York and Clarence Thornton were on the city council . . . if we could have kept them forever, Reno would have been some sort of a place! These guys were dedicated, hard working, hard thinking, practical guys, and it was during their administration that Reno made the greatest strides.

But Barbara Bennett . . . I called her one day—there was a big hoorah going on over the tax exempt securities that cities and counties and municipalities issued. Congress was considering making them taxable. I said, "Mayor, this bill before Congress is going to cost the city of Reno a lot of money."

She said, "Why?"

Well," I said, "the reason you sell them so quick is that you can sell them under the current market price because there's no tax on them. If they become taxable, you're going have to . . . ."

And she said, "Smith, I don't understand a thing you're talking about. Would you mind calling up my finance director and explaining it to him?"

I said, "Yeah, Mayor, I would object to doing that. If you really want him to know, ask him to call me." [laughter] He never did.

Barbara Bennett was a "no-growth" advocate and she brought a lot of votes with her, but people didn't understand what they were voting for, and it's too bad. It's like, why do all the minorities vote for welfare? If they had to work and pay taxes and see that they were paying for this sort of thing, their attitude would probably change, and change quickly.

Barbara's political philosophy, as I understand it, was that we don't need successful people around; we don't want them around. But Reno has *always* been provincial in its thinking. Reno wanted to be like San Francisco, while Las Vegas tried to copy southern California for a long time: "Let her go; let her rip! Let's get down the road to the next thing." And who is to say one is right and one is wrong? One's the last frontier and one wants to be provincial. When I was a kid, women were still wearing gloves when they went out at night in Reno. It's just an attitude that Reno's always had.

# 21

*Real Outlaws*

THE GUYS WHO WERE holding up banks in the old days were tough guys; I mean, they were real outlaws! A. R. Collins, one of our managers, was actually shot in a hold-up of Bank of Nevada. Ray Collins was a character. You couldn't make him mad if you spit on him, hit him, cussed him; but if he saw someone stealing, he absolutely went berserk. He couldn't control himself.

Before coming to Las Vegas Ray worked as a branch manager for Bank of America down in the L. A. area. They'd had a lot of hold-ups down there, so he'd carried a pistol and kept a deer rifle under the counter. He told me, "Once a guy came in and stuck a gun to my head. He took me back to the vault and put me down on my knees and told me to open the safe. As I started to work on it he put his gun in his pocket, so I just reached around and pulled my pistol out and shot him." He said, "Another guy robbed us and jumped in his car, and I ran out with my deer rifle and shot his tires out as he was starting down the road." [laughter] He'd been in eleven or twelve robberies before the one in Las Vegas.

Ray was the manager at the main office of the Bank of Nevada when it was at First and Carson, and when this robbery began to unfold he set off the silent alarms. When the robber left, Ray followed him. The guy went out and down the alley, and he walked through the Golden Nugget and out to the corner. The traffic light was against him, so he stood there, and Ray came up behind him and said, "Hey, partner, why don't you come back to the bank with me and put that money back where you took it from?" And the guy pulled a gun and shot Ray; didn't kill him, but hurt him bad. Shot his intestines up. Then the guy ran down the street half a block, got in his car, stuck the gun to his head and killed himself. Ray recovered, but he was never physically well again.

There was no real bank security in Nevada back when I got started. But once crime increased and we got more hold-ups and so forth, into the late 1950s and early 1960s, people started to say, "Hey, wait a minute!" First we put in silent alarms, and then came the cameras. In the old days they were film; now they're videotape. We always had guards, but I'm not sure a guard does any good for security at a bank. In fact, unless he's well trained a guard may just create some problems. Most of them are senior citizens who are good at opening the door for customers, but they aren't what you really need if you're expecting armed robbery and that sort of stuff.

The most important thing the banks have done to discourage robberies is that they've learned how to manage their cash better. On pay days down at the old Sparks branch it was nothing for a teller to have a hundred thousand dollars in his drawer—we were cashing those railroad pay checks all day long. But now if you rob a teller and take everything she has, you're lucky to get fifteen hundred, because tellers operate with a minimum of cash in their drawers; and when they take in big bills, these go where they can't get them back. Plus, there are cameras all over the place, taking pictures of everything that's going on, and silent alarms are going off at the police station, and you hand the robber a bundle of money that explodes when he goes through the door and covers him with indelible ink. Robbing banks just ain't worth the aggravation anymore! [laughter]

The exploding money looks like a stack of twenty-dollar bills. It isn't. There's a phony twenty on each side, and there's a pouch of indelible ink in it and a little explosive device. When you pull the stack from the drawer to hand it to the guy, it arms itself. Once it's armed, if it passes through the magnetic field in the doors, it explodes. It isn't going to kill a robber, but it blows indelible ink all over him. He's a mess. Everybody knows who he is—he can't say, "It wasn't me!"

Those sorts of things really cut back on robberies. Today the typical bank robber is a drunk who wants another beer, so he goes into a bank and sticks a gun in a teller's face and says, "Give me your money." [laughter] But extortions are another matter. I went through I don't know how many extortion attempts. We even had a kidnapping once in the early 1970s:

Polly Possum had been a country and western singer. She was married to the manager of our Las Vegas main branch, a guy named Reno Fruzza. (He had grown up on Sixth and E Streets in Sparks.) One evening Fruzza came home and there were two guys standing in his driveway. They said, "Come on, you're going in the house. We have Polly." They took him in and they said, "Tomorrow morning we're going to take your wife away and give her a shot—an injection of something that will kill her in sixteen hours if she doesn't get the antidote."

The next morning they disappeared with Polly. Then they came back and said, "Now, if you want your wife to live, go down to the bank and get two million dollars. Then go over to a phone booth on Third Street, where you'll find a note that will tell you what to do with the money." So Fruzza went to the bank and took over a million bucks from the vault and jumped in his car. Even though he's the manager, while he's taking the money from the vault someone from the bank figures something goofy's going on, so they call the FBI. By the time the FBI got there he'd left. He'd gone over to this phone booth, and there's a note that says, "Drive your car out to the covered parking lot at the Sahara Hotel. There you'll find an old . . . (I forget what it was— Buick, Cadillac or something.) There's an orange stripe

174

on the trunk and the keys are under the mat. There'll be a note in the car for you."

The note directed him down a dirt road way out into the desert, and told him where he would find a big rock with an orange mark on it. Under the rock would be more instructions. They really had him going. Finally, after driving four or five hours down through Sandy Valley, he ends up at Pahrump with the money in the trunk of his car. He was supposed to go to a certain bar and wait for a call for a name they had given him. While he's waiting he hears an airplane land; after a few minutes it takes off again. He kept waiting and waiting, and no call. Finally he went out to look around, checked the trunk, and the money was gone. It was like a Hollywood movie. A note in the trunk said his wife was in a room at the Show Boat Hotel—she was safe; she didn't need any antidote. The crooks had rented an airplane out at Sky Harbor in North Las Vegas, flown up to Pahrump, took the money out of the trunk, got in the airplane and flew back. The FBI finally tracked them down and caught them a few years later.

We had a lot of extortion attempts—more back then than now. Finally we said, "Look, we know how to count money but we don't know how to prevent crime." So we went out and found Vern Loetterle. He had been in charge of the FBI in Alaska; then he was special agent in charge of the Nevada office, and then he planned to retire after a stint in Arizona. I asked him to become the head of our security when he retired, and he did.

Vern Loetterle was probably one of the best things that ever happened to FNB. He saw to it that if the crooks were going to get us, it wasn't going to be easy. In the 1970s, right after the Fruzza incident, he had me start carrying a snub-nosed Smith & Wesson .38 special. (I had a little holster that fit on my hip right inside my belt.) He also put radios in all of our cars. My car was rigged so I could open the trunk door from the inside if I was locked into it, and he put a light in there and a .357 magnum hidden in a compartment. The idea was that if crooks stuff me in my trunk and drive away with me, the first time they hit a stop sign I've already turned the light on and found the gun. I hit the button and the lid goes up and I jump out. [laughter] We had that in all our cars.

He also would just give me hell if I drove to work the same way every day. One day I'm at home and I see this guy in a car out front taking pictures. I wonder what the hell is going on, so I call security and say "Is Loetterle there?"

"No."

I said, "I'll try to get him on the radio." (My call sign was 001 and Ernie Martinelli was 002. Loetterle was 007.) [laughter]

I said, "Double ought seven, this is double ought one."

He said, "Go ahead."

I said, "There's a strange car out in front of my house, and a guy is taking photographs from it."

He said, "My, you're alert. It's me."

"It isn't your car."

He said, "Right! I just wanted to see if you were paying attention." [laughter]

Later at a management seminar of the presidents of all our affiliated banks, Loetterle gave a presentation on security. He said, "Let me show you something," and he's got all these photographs of my house, the different ways out. "Nine times out of ten," he said, "Art will go out this way. If I'm a bank robber and I want to take him hostage, I'm only going to miss him one day out of ten. You don't have to drive to work the same way every morning. You don't have to leave at five minutes to nine every morning either."

I was lucky—no one ever tried anything with me. However, one morning Ernie Martinelli, our president, got a phone call. A voice said, "We got your daughter. Go over to that pay phone at Ben's Liquor Store at Fourth and Keystone and wait for a call." We called the FBI, and Ernie went over and stayed at that pay phone. Pretty soon the FBI called back and reported that all three of Ernie's daughters were secure, so he didn't have to worry. It was just a cruel hoax.

We were getting so many extortion attempts and threats that Vern started putting panic alarms in the houses of our branch managers—all you had to do was hit the alarm and the police knew that there was an extortion going on. The best place to put a panic alarm is in the bathroom, because if someone comes and sticks a gun in your face, the first thing you say is, "Oh, my God, I've got to pee!" And they'll let you go pee.

177

When you do, you just reach under the toilet and set the alarm off.

We had another alarm system that activated microphones in your ceiling when you turned it on. The wife of one of our branch managers in Las Vegas had to use their panic alarm—it had the microphone setup. She said, "What are you going to do with me?" They said, "We're going to take you to a parking lot at the El Rancho. We'll turn you loose when your husband brings the money out." And the police were listening to all this. They caught them.

Vern went on to design practically all of the First Interstate Bank security systems throughout the West. Some of it was pretty sophisticated stuff. For instance, we had to get permits from the F.C.C. to transmit on a dish from Second and Virginia to First and Virginia and then from First and Virginia to our warehouse and security offices down on Vassar Street. You could go in Vern's central security control room at any time and he could tell you everything that was going on everywhere. You could look at anything you wanted to. We hired a real pro.

Vern Loetterle did wonders for our security. If nothing else, he made it a part of our thoughts every day. You were aware of security; and if you weren't, he'd see to it that you became aware of it. He taught us that security is something like . . . you have to sweep the floor every morning and you have to think about security every morning, too. You don't just think about it when something happens.

# 22

## *Gambling Couldn't Be Tolerated*

WHEN I LEFT LAS VEGAS in 1968 I was succeeded as president of Bank of Nevada by Alex Sample. Alex had been a national bank examiner before going to work for a bank that was owned by Transamerica in Kalispell, Montana. He eventually became the head guy.

When Western Bancorp moved me to Reno they said, "Who do you think ought to replace you?"

I said, "Alex Sample."

"Why don't you go up and ask him if he wants to move to Nevada?"

I said, "Why should I ask him? I don't run the holding company." [laughter]

"Well," they said, "Go up and ask him anyway."

Of course, he accepted the job. He was the last president of Bank of Nevada before it was merged with First National of Nevada. Alex was a damned good banker and a great guy, but he got in trouble with booze, and that took him down. The holding company eventually had to fire him.

I have seen it so many times—some of the best guys come into Nevada and they can't handle it. They can't handle the gaming; they can't handle the booze; they can't handle the girls. They'd be perfect in San Francisco, but two years in Nevada and they're bums. And it's not their fault. I mean, it's just . . . .

Gambling couldn't be tolerated. When you gamble and lose and you run out of money, there's always the temptation to . . . . When you're a banker, you're where the money is. I've seen so many guys—Red O'Leary, the whole bunch of them—they'd get caught in some big defalcation in the bank, and when you got down to the root of it, they'd gambled and lost and they stole.

At the old Bank of Nevada we had a rule that if you got caught gambling you were fired. Employees signed a statement acknowledging that neither they nor their family could gamble, couldn't even pull a slot machine handle. The wife of one of my top guys got addicted to the slots, and I finally had to call him in and tell him, "Look, you know what the rule is and Helen knows what the rule is. You tell Helen the next time *she* pulls a handle on a slot machine, *you're* fired!"

When I was running Bank of Nevada I reported to Gay Prather, a fellow in the holding company who had gone to bat for me to make me president of the bank. Everyone had said, "Smith's too young," but Prather had said, "He isn't either; let's give him a chance." He fought for me and got me the job. Later he transferred into the First National Bank and became a high officer in the bank in southern Nevada. I think he and Eddie Questa had a deal that when Eddie retired, Gay would become head of FNB of Nevada.

Well, Gay Prather was one of my closest friends, but a couple of things happened that finally destroyed the friendship. When he went to FNB he suddenly became my competitor from daylight to dark—he was the enemy across the street. Then when I became president and CEO of First National Bank, it was a total surprise to him. He thought *he* was in line, and I never told him that I was going. Nobody told him. Then one day the bank announced that Bert Fitz had retired and Gorman was going to retire next May and Art Smith had been picked to run the bank. (I will never forget the headlines in the paper in Reno: "First National Picks Las Vegan.")

For a time after I became chairman, I thought that maybe I would make Gay president, put him in Reno, and I could go back and live in southern Nevada. I brought the idea to some of our board members, and the Las Vegas board member said, "No. We don't think he's right for it." So that's when Ernie Martinelli became president and Gay was given another title, which at least put him among the top guys in FNB of Nevada.

One day I got a tip that Gay was gambling, but I didn't pay too much attention to it. I thought, "He knows better than that." Then I get a phone call from Moe Dalitz. Moe says, "Art, I loaned Gay some money for gambling and he hasn't paid me back. How am I going to get it back?"

I called Gay in. He denied that he was gambling. I said, "But Gay, you *can't* deny it when Moe Dalitz calls and tells me that you owe him money. I'm not here to tell you to pay Moe back, but you know you can't work here and gamble. You know that." And he said, "I know it."

Then we have a convention of the Nevada Bankers Association up at Lake Tahoe and I find out the next morning that he stayed up all night gambling and lost twenty-five hundred or so. I talked to Cliff Tweter, the president of the holding company. I said, "Cliff, this is just against everything we do over here in Nevada, and Gay Prather knows it. If he doesn't get it straightened out I have no choice but to let him go. Now, he's really your guy to start with, so I don't want it to be a surprise to you." Cliff said, "If you have to, you have to."

Finally I was in my office in Reno one day when I got a call from an officer in the bank in Las Vegas. He said, "If you want to know where Prather is right now, he's out at Caesar's Palace playing Twenty-one." I jumped on an airplane, and when I hit Las Vegas I took a cab over to Caesar's Palace, and there he was, still playing Twenty-one. I just stood off twenty or thirty feet behind him, and people got that sense, you know . . . . All of a sudden he looked back and saw me; cashed in and came over. I said, "Well, Gay, you know what the story is." He said, "OK," and we went down to the bank and he handed me his keys and left. And this was the

182

guy who had made me the president of the Bank of Nevada. Gay Prather, in my opinion, had become a compulsive gambler. He was as sick with it as an alcoholic is with booze.

You couldn't gamble and you couldn't be a heavy drinker, and there were one or two other things that could cost you your job. There were also some things you were expected to do if you wanted to keep it—if you were an officer in one of the branches or anywhere, you were expected to be community minded and community active.

A guy named Bill Wilkie was running the Bank of Nevada then. He was a pretty capable guy, but he didn't want to get involved with anything, period. His board of directors told him one day in a meeting, "Bill, if you don't get involved in the community here in Las Vegas, we're going to talk to the holding company and see if we can't get someone who will get involved."

When we merged the Bank of Nevada with the First National Bank we had two executive levels, and one was going to disappear. You don't need two. So when we talked about bringing people over on the merger, someone said, "What about Wilkie?" And I said, "There's no place over here for Wilkie." I just knew that here was a guy that was not going to be involved. He used to bring his lunch to work and close his office door and sit and eat lunch at his desk; and not because he was trying to be frugal or wanted to save money. In fact, he told his board, "If you expect me to be out running around making a lot of noise and pumping up the bank, you got the wrong guy." He had a good personality; he just didn't want to get involved.

# 23

---

## *Retired, but Still in the Building*

RIGHT AFTER I BECAME PRESIDENT of FNB we moved Ernie Martinelli up from cashier to be my administrative vice president. He was very helpful. I had been away from Reno for twenty-two years, and he helped me renew contacts and this sort of thing, and he became almost my alter ego. Then about 1973 we underwent a slight reorganization. I was a long way from retiring, but we started talking about succession in the bank, and putting it in order. We decided that Ernie should become president and I'd remain chairman and CEO. I also brought up Gary Updegraf, planning eventually to make him the chief financial officer of the bank. He was real good, and he brought another guy along with him as his assistant, Ron Zurek. They set up an outstanding financial department; nobody's was better. The bank's future looked good, but then around 1981 our holding company made a personnel decision that backfired.

Bill Siart was a young man, in his mid thirties, very ambitious and moving up. He had gone through the Bank of America's junior executive training program and he had worked in the holding company as a marketing guy; he had had an opportunity to look at all the different banks and see what was going on. At the time, we were the best performing bank in the whole system— any way you wanted to look at it, in our peer group of a hundred banks we always ranked in the top one or two. A couple of years before I was ready to retire Siart convinced his pal Joe Pinola, the head of Western Bancorp, to send him over to be president of First Interstate of Nevada, with the idea that he would succeed me as chairman when I stepped down.

My plan had been to retire in 1987 when I expected Ernie Martinelli to succeed me as chief executive officer of the bank, so I tried to talk Pinola out of sending Siart to Reno. It was like talking to a stop sign. Pinola was really on an ego trip, and he did lots of foolish things. He was one of these guys who had never run a bank. He thought he had, because he had run the North American division of Bank of America; but when you're the head of a division like that you're not running a bank—you're kind of like the head personnel officer.

So Bill Siart came to Reno, and he proved to be a disrupting presence. To make room for him Ernie Martinelli was moved to Las Vegas and made a vice chairman; but Ernie couldn't get along with Bill, and eventually he quit to become president and chairman of Security Bank in Reno. When he did, Ernie took Buzzy

Allen along with him as his operating guy. Gary Updegraf and Ron Zurek also quit. We lost some real good guys there . . . in fact, there was a lot of turnover during Siart's short time at the bank. I think it created morale problems, but how do you measure morale?

As Siart got more authority, he wanted to bring in his own guys. He brought in one out of First Interstate of California to be our senior credit officer, but all the guy did was talk. And man, he talked! You'd think he'd invented credit, but when we looked and saw how many loans he had made, the number was zero. The guys in the bank quickly got wise to him: he was really more of a credit review guy than a senior credit officer. Instead of helping and counseling with the loans, he would sit and tell you all the mistakes you made after you made them.

Another of Siart's guys was Dick Petty. Ernie Martinelli and I had hired him to run personnel, but the minute that Bill Siart arrived Petty became his henchman. Bill would run roughshod over anybody if he thought it would help him, and anything that Bill wanted done, Petty was the guy who went out and did it for him. The guys gave him the nickname "Petty Dick." [laughter] His other nickname was "The Brave Buzzard." Of course, he left the bank when Siart moved on a couple of years later.

For some reason Joe Pinola didn't like Harry Fletcher, the guy who was running southern Nevada for us. He ordered me and Ernie Martinelli to fire him. We resisted, but it got to the point where Pinola said, "Well, if you guys won't get rid of him, I'm going to send Siart down to do it." And we said, "Just a minute, Joe, he's our friend and we've worked with him forever and we're not going to let some young guy go down and fire him. If he has to be fired, if that's what you want, we'll do it." We did it, but we made it perfectly plain to Fletcher that it wasn't our idea.

Bill Siart was actually a pretty bright guy, but I sometimes questioned his ethics. For instance, he bought a tuxedo and put it on his expense account with the notation that it was for bank use only. I refused to sign his expense account, so he went and made someone else do it. There were always questionable trans-actions . . . . If you were transferred and couldn't sell your house, the bank would appraise it and buy it and make you whole, but the rule was very specific: it had to be your principal residence. We saw one of those deals go through on Bill's house, and when we finally traced it down and got to the bottom of it, it was for a house that he had as rental property over in Orinda, and not his principal residence in Manhattan Beach. You just questioned why he did things like that.

Siart had no street sense, absolutely none. One day he and Hank Gallues and I were in a meeting and we got to talking about something that Siart couldn't under-stand, and he said, "If there's anything I can't under-stand, you give me a book about it; and I'll read it, and by the next day I'll understand exactly what's going on."

Hank said to him, "I tell you what I'm going to do, Bill. I'm going to give you a book on how to swim. Then tomorrow I'm going to throw you in the swimming pool and we'll see how it works." Bill came into my office and asked me what Hank meant by that. [laughter]

When Bill took over he wanted us to operate under a theory that he had read in some book: he wanted our bank to be "customer driven." I'm not exactly sure what that meant, but it turned out that he let customers kind of do as they pleased in certain instances, and the bank put out some loans that turned into terrible losses. After Siart left, when the bank foreclosed on some of these loans they found that they were greater than the appraised value of the property. In one case the difference was in the millions of dollars. I don't know if that's being customer driven or what it is, but the bank had some real rough times credit-wise for a while. Whether it was entirely Siart's fault or not, he was the boss at the time, and if you're the boss it's your problem. I guess I'm biased, but a lot of people at the bank felt the same way.

During the first couple of years Siart was in Reno I was still the chairman and CEO, so theoretically I could exercise some control over him. But he had been sent to us by his pal Joe Pinola, and every time there was a difference of opinion he'd say, "Well, I'll just call Joe and straighten it out." It was always, "You're the boss, but I'm wired up to headquarters and we'll handle it my way." He was really part of the reason that I retired at age sixty-two rather than at sixty-five. I had my full pension in, and staying another three years wouldn't get me any more. Why put up with the aggravation? I just said, "Let him do what he wants; I'm out of here." And then a year later he was gone too, leaving a mess behind.

I retired in 1984 after twenty-four years as a CEO, the first eight with Bank of Nevada. That's too long! I had gotten bored, and, without realizing it, I'd stopped giving everything I had. Once I had the bank running like a sewing machine . . . you know, "if it ain't broke, don't fix it," but that doesn't mean that you can't make it run better. We had brought the bank up to close to three billion dollars in deposits, but the job had become routine, just like getting up and brushing your teeth. And if there were challenges out there . . . when you're sixty-two years old you've had enough challenges. [laughter]

When I announced my retirement four directors individually came to me and said, "Art, is this your idea or is this the holding company's idea? Because if it's the holding company's idea we're not going to let it happen."

I said, "No, it's strictly my idea."

Pinola didn't know I was going to do it until I told Siart, and then Siart burned the rug up getting to his office to call him and tell him "Smith's retiring!"

I was retiring, but I wasn't leaving the building. I was given a small office on the twelfth floor. You'd think Siart would've let me have a little time to move out of my old office, but while I'm trying to get out, he's in there pressuring me. We all had identical desks, and he said, "Just take the drawers out of that desk and put them in the one upstairs, and bring the upstairs drawers down and put them in this desk." I wasn't even out of the office and he was moving in; he couldn't wait! [laughter] I think he had an insecure feeling that until he got in that office he was never going to be the boss.

Even though I was retired, I wasn't ready to just quit and sit in a rocking chair, and the bank treated me well and found things for me to do. I'm occasionally asked to advise or assist on projects, and Larry Tuntland, the president since 1991, has kept me involved socially. If there's something going on and he has a table of eight or ten, he'll say, "Why don't you and Charlotte come to this?" I know a lot of people in Nevada (some of them like me and some of them don't), and I can still repre sent the bank at places where it wants to be represented.

# 24

---

## *It Wasn't a Job, It Was Just Fun*

IN COMPLEXION AND PERSONALITY I take after the Scandinavian side of my family. I'm like my mother—I'm the one with the short fuse and the "let's get it done now, not when we're older" attitude. I'm also kind of compulsive: When I started to build model airplanes, before I knew it I'd built twenty; when I decided to blow the horn, instead of practicing one hour a day I practiced five hours a day; and when I decided to be a ham radio operator, I got my license in about two months. Jumping around, never staying with anything . . . .

I would usually stay with something only until I didn't want to learn anything more about it, and then I'd move on to something else. That almost happened with banking. My first experience with banking was not terribly exciting, and I had no intention of going back into it after the war. When I did anyway, I didn't think I'd last long. It just wasn't my cup of tea. I started in operations, and I was never a guy who really loved operations—I wanted to be on the loan side and the public relations side and that sort of thing, and when I eventually decided to stay with banking, that's where I went. Soon I had a nice little career going, and when I finally got to be the boss . . . yes! [laughter] Life is good when you're the boss and in a position to control the destiny of your company to a certain extent.

There was something else that kept me in banking, and that's competition. I'm damned competitive. You begin to compete, and you want to win, and you aren't going to win anything if you get out. When I started at the Bank of Nevada there was a guy there named Vern Waldo. He'd been a school teacher in Wyoming, an athletic director or a coach, I guess, and he was very ambitious. I was younger, but I had had some banking experience, and we soon developed a little rivalry. Vern left when we were both junior officers—he went up to First National in Reno to become the cashier, which in those days was the chief operating officer. He kind of laughed at me when he took off. He said, "See you later, pal." When I became the president of the whole outfit in 1967, he came into my office, and I said, "Are you still the cashier?" [laughter]

I'm a firm believer that you can have too many people reporting to you. Some guys would say, "You know how many guys I got reporting to me? Thirty!" And I'd say, "Well, then, nobody's *reporting* to you." [laughter] When I was CEO I had only four guys reporting to me: the marketing guy, the credit guy, the operating guy, and Ernie Martinelli.

No matter how many people report to you, you have to handle them right to get the most out of them. When I became president of the Bank of Nevada, the chairman of our holding company was Frank L. King, and his president was Clifford Tweter. Quarterly, the presidents of the twenty-three banks would meet with Tweter in a huge board room around a big table. He treated all of us the same. His philosophy was that he expected us to run the banks on a day-to-day basis, but that if we had a problem and asked for help, he would do all he could for us. If we didn't ask for help we were on our own: "Do as you damned well please. If you get problems, let's work them out together; if you go it alone, you suffer the consequences." Joe Pinola was the exact opposite—he loved to intimidate. I heard him say many times, "Let me tell you guys something: I could replace any one of you, and six weeks from now nobody would even remember who you were." With that attitude he sent young guys off to places where they didn't make it. Pinola was a hip shooter who made bad decisions, and he almost wrecked the company a couple of times.

I leaned more toward persuasion and cooperation than toward autocratic decisions. John DeLuca was an old friend who was the biggest liquor distributor in southern Nevada. (He had been a bootlegger before prohibition.) John had a little plaque on his desk that said, "All of us are smarter than any one of us," and I've always felt that way. I might know more about playing marbles than you do, but you know a hell of a lot more about writing a book than I do. We get different kinds of people together and we get the best of all us. The same principle applies to boards of directors. When I was running FIB of Nevada we would have only two insiders on our board. Why do you need more? The insiders can tell the board what's going on in the bank and what the bank wants to do and why it wants to do it; and if you have a special problem you can call in a specialist to advise you. On boards that are dominated by insiders, you know that however the chairman votes, that's how the other insiders are going to vote. No insider's going to say, "Mr. Chairman, you're crazy!" So you're really giving the chairman sole control if you let him have more insiders than he's got outsiders. Do it the other way, and the guy says, "You want to buy a computer, Smith? Tell me why."

Even with members from a variety of backgrounds, here's the way a typical board of directors or executive committee works: Say there's a proposal to buy a ten million dollar computer system. Only one member of the committee understands computers, and he's afraid that if he says anything the other guys will think he's a smartass. So he says nothing, and they pass on it in about two minutes, spend the ten million bucks. Then they get down to buying dishes for the staff room. Some of them know a little bit about this, so it takes thirty-five minutes discussion before they buy five hundred dollars worth of dishes. Now they consider buying a bicycle for the bank messenger. *Everybody* knows about bicycles. [laughter] So they spend an hour talking about it before they buy a bike. That's the way a lot of those things work.

I was dead set against some of the things that A. P. Giannini did with Transamerica. Giannini was a fine man with a social conscience, and he wanted his banks to take care of the masses, but I'm not sure that he went about it the right way. He and his son and their successors seemed to think that big for the sake of bigness was good: "We're getting bigger, and we got more branches and more people than any other bank," . . . that sort of thing. Transamerica also had a reputation for underpaying their people horribly—you had to starve to work for them. It was only when the real technological advances came, and Transamerica and Western Bancorp hired guys who were experts in science and technology, that the big mess of banks and branches that Giannini had put together really began to run as top-drawer banks in a top-drawer system.

With our bank, the whole state of Nevada was our community. We were as concerned about the rancher in Elko as we were about the automobile dealer in Las Vegas or the guy selling clothes in Reno. Of course, banks should try to improve life in the areas where they operate, and there were ways for us to make things happen other than just through encouraging savings and making loans to everybody—a bank can have a huge influence on the quality of life in the community it serves by providing leadership and by giving financial support to worthy projects. It seemed obvious to me that the more successful you can make a community, the more successful your bank's going to be; but in today's business environment some bankers seem to have lost track of that fact, and the days when banks would give huge sums of money to civic improvement may be over. Now there is immense pressure from the top to "stop wasting money" and to increase earnings for the shareholders at all costs: "We don't care how you do it; just do it." I didn't have to deal with that kind of pressure when I was running the bank.

Motivation is critical to success in any organization, and the best way to motivate people is by example. If you want to sit in your office all morning long and read the *Wall Street Journal*, then your people will think they're supposed to sit in their offices and read the *Wall Street Journal*. You should always be involved. You're doing this; you're doing that; you're going here; you're going there; and it builds up enthusiasm and energy. I mean, "Jesus, let's get going! Let's get going!" Or you hear about a new idea and you say, "Why does this work in Utah and it won't work here?" You talk about it, and before long you get people all stirred up, and they say, "We can make it work here." Hell, in the old days everybody that I was associated with could hardly wait for the sun to come up so we could go down to the bank and go to work. We enjoyed it that much. It wasn't a job; it was just fun.

For people of my generation, life in general may have been a little bit more relaxed, a bit more fun than it is today. I think that was due in large part to the fact that you could get along and raise a family comfortably on one salary. Charlotte wanted to stay home and raise our kids, and I wanted her to, and it was better for the kids and easier for both of us—our nights and weekends weren't spent trying to catch up on things that hadn't gotten done on weekdays. Unfortunately, few married people with children live that way anymore. Nobody's better off when a mother also has to be a breadwinner, but the average family can't make it on one salary today.

There are other reasons why I believe I've lived during the best period in our history. They start with the war: if there can be such a thing as a good war, World War II was it for the United States. We fought for the right reasons, we won, and we came out of the war filled with confidence and a desire to get things done. None of us feared anything—we were certain that the future was bright, and it was! Beginning in the late 1940s, there was such growth and prosperity . . . and then there were the medical and technological advances: penicillin was introduced, polio was wiped out, computers changed our lives, we went to the moon . . . . What other generation has seen such progress?

I was born in the age of steam, but there I was at Cape Kennedy watching men climb aboard Apollo 11 to head for the moon. They took off, and we got in the car and started driving back to Orlando. We had the radio on, and when we were still seventy-five miles from Orlando we heard that the astronauts had orbited the earth twice, fired their rockets, and were on their way to the moon. The difference between the steam engines of my youth, which were marvels of their time, and a moon rocket boggles my mind—when I was a boy, I wouldn't have believed that men would walk on the moon before I was fifty years old. My life and career have been just as surprising to me, seeming to unfold almost without any planning, from being raised in a railroad family during the Great Depression to running one of the most successful banks in the West.

In a life filled with good fortune, my greatest luck was to have Charlotte for my wife. Together we've had the best of times, and we have four wonderful kids and ten happy, healthy grandchildren. How could things have gone any better?

# Appendix

*Some Reflections on Banking*
*The Way It Was*

FORTY-THREE YEARS PASSED between the day I started in banking and the day I retired. During those four decades the fundamental business of banking didn't change appreciably, but the way it was done was utterly transformed. The biggest changes stemmed from the development and introduction of computers. All we had when I started were adding machines, and they weren't even electrical; but although you pulled them by hand, they never made a mistake. [laughter] Where we used to post ledgers and statements manually, now it's all done by high-speed computers and high-speed printers, and checks are sorted on high-speed sorters. Back in the 'forties and 'fifties a good bookkeeper could handle eight hundred to a thousand accounts, but the convention hall in Reno wouldn't hold all the oldtime bookkeepers you'd need to do what's being done by computers at FIB today.

When I was at the Sparks branch of the First National in 1941 and '42 our normal hours of business were ten o'clock till three, and we were open on Saturdays from ten till noon. The theory was that if you didn't stay open on Saturday, how was the poor farmer ever going to come in and get his business done? Now, the fact of the matter is, the farmer is the only guy who can come in any day he wants. [laughter]

On Southern Pacific paydays, which were twice a month, we opened an hour early and stayed open an hour late, and the workers would cash thousands of paychecks. It was absolutely . . . it was organized mayhem, is what it was. Block-long lines of men waiting to cash their checks—we'd open the bank's doors in the morning, and here they'd come! In order to have enough cash to operate the whole day, we'd have stacks of bills stashed everywhere. We'd have fifteen thousand dollars in twenties in a wastebasket, and ten thousand in fives lying over here, and . . . our drawers were just full of cash!

By the end of the day we'd be out of cash, and we'd have stacks and stacks of cashed checks. These were what we called transient checks, all drawn on a bank in San Francisco where the Southern Pacific had its headquarters. Our branch couldn't afford a Recordak, so we had to take the transient checks up to the Reno main office to have them photographed before we could mail them. (A Recordak was a device which took pictures of a check front and back, so that if it got lost when you sent it by mail to the Fed or to the bank in San Francisco, you had evidence and you didn't lose the money.)

We balanced every day, and come New Year's we balanced the bank for the year. At the end of 1941, we didn't do it the next working day; we did the whole thing on New Year's Eve! We started balancing in the evening, and then we all went down to the Lincoln Hotel and had dinner and came back. We finished before midnight, and we had the bank balanced for the whole year—all the totals were there. All this with adding machines, strictly adding machines with tapes.

The branch's total assets were just nine hundred and eighty thousand; and if you even mentioned that number outside the bank, they fired you. [laughter] And the profit made each month: the general ledger bookkeeper and the manager saw that figure, nobody else. That was the deepest, darkest secret in the world. Today you couldn't even open the door with such limited assets, but back then we were the only bank in Sparks.

The manager of the Sparks branch was a guy named Joe Sbragia. Jay Lockridge was one of my friends at the bank—his father used to be chief of police in Sparks. Then there was Art Chlopeck, an oldtimer who really helped me become a teller and taught me to post the general ledger. He worked for the bank up until he died. And Dave Tarner, Dick Bradbury, Pauline Lillard, Louise Oborn . . . we were like a little family, and once you got into the routines it was just a job.

We'd come in at eight o'clock in the morning, and between eight and ten, when we opened for business, a lot of work went on. We had big savings ledgers that tracked all the savings accounts; same thing with the checking accounts; same thing with cashier's checks. To prove a ledger, you'd add up all the entries individually to see if they balanced to the control sheet that was in the front. If they didn't, you had to go back and see if you had mislisted one. If there wasn't a mislisting on the adding machine, then you had to go back and cross check—get all the savings deposits and withdrawals since the last proof, and physically see that they were posted correctly by hand.

Then to proof the cashier's checks you took all the outstanding checks, the ones you had issued but which hadn't come in yet, to see if you got the right liabilities there. If they all came in, you'd have enough money—you wouldn't have too much, you wouldn't have too little. After ten o'clock in the morning it was mostly balancing up the batch sheets and posting the checking accounts, the ledgers. We'd get the bank balanced in the afternoon, and then in the morning we'd start over and do the whole thing again. You spent a lot of time keeping the bank in balance.

When I started I posted only the ledgers; they wouldn't let me post the statements, because there could be no corrections on statements. You could correct a ledger by taking it to one of the officers of the bank and saying, "I made this mistake. Here's the check, and here's the correction," and he'd initial it. But statements had to be letter perfect. You didn't want to go to an officer and admit to a mistake on a statement.

Then I started running what they called batch sheets. That's how they kept the bank balanced. On one side you would list all the debits, and all the credits would be on the other side. You'd have savings deposits and checking deposits and cashier check applications and that sort of thing on one side, and on the other side you'd have whatever the offset was—a check or cash or some sort of a credit memo. It was a little hard for me originally, because in a bank the accounting is all the opposite of what you think it should be. You make a deposit, and that's an *asset* for you; but the bank accepts your deposit, and that's a *liability* for them because they owe it to you. They increase an asset, a loan, by lending your deposit, a debit! After learning straight accounting and math in high school and college, all of a sudden I'm having to remember that an asset is a liability. [laughter]

Here's how it worked: I'm a batch clerk, and a teller gets his drawer full of paper, so I go over and take it from him. I take what's in his window, but I don't take any cash, because he's either got a cash ticket which says he got so much cash in this deposit, or he checked it off on the deposit slip. I just take the paperwork. So I have a record of all the commercial deposits, savings deposits, loan payments, cashier check applications, and all this. Instead of just being at random, as they came in, now I put them in categories and enter a grand total at the bottom. Over here I got a check from Southern Pacific Railroad, which is a transit check. It's one that isn't going to be paid in our bank; it's one that will be collected in San Francisco. Then you got the checks which are drawn on us—we issued a check and you brought it in and deposited it with us. Then there's the cash. And then there could be postal money orders.

The batch clerk put everything in categories and totaled them. The left side had to equal the right, or something was wrong. You cross checked to try to get it in balance. At the end of the day they took all of the batch sheets and made a final top batch sheet, which was a consolidation of all this. Those are the numbers that went into the general ledger.

I could post checking account ledgers, but not the general ledger. In those days the general ledger was posted by hand—liabilities were in black ink, and assets were posted in red. You had to balance the ledger every day, and if you ran the batch sheet, which was ultimately the final entries that got into the general ledger, they wouldn't let you post the general ledger because you could control what went into it.

After I learned how to do batch sheets, they started training me to be a teller. Back then a teller took savings and checking deposits, booked cashier checks, took loan payments . . . did everything at that one window. (It wasn't like a few years ago when a commercial teller didn't do anything but take checking and savings deposits, period! But banking has come full circle, and now tellers are doing everything again.) Finally they taught you to post the general ledger.

When you could post the general ledger, you were as capable as you could be without becoming some sort of a junior officer. But you couldn't post the loan boards. Only an officer could do that. Every loan that went on the books was posted on a big loan board, telling what the percentage was, the maturity, the payment schedule, and all these things. It was balanced each day, and went into batches, and finally the information got into the general ledger.

In those days if you started in a small branch, when you got through you'd done everything, and you'd make a great operations officer in any bank; but you wouldn't know anything about the lending function. There are two functions in a bank: operations (taking deposits, posting them, keeping the bank in balance) and lending. For some reason the lending side is supposed to be the dramatic side. They're the fighter pilots, and these guys over here in operations are the tank drivers, slogging through, keeping everything in order and in balance.

When I was at the Sparks branch I wasn't on the lending side, but you could see who they were lending to and how they were doing it. It was pretty simple. The bank built up credit files on borrowers, and if they had more assets than liabilities, and they had a reputation for honesty, they could borrow. Otherwise, "Get out of here!" Nothing very sophisticated, and everything was short term compared to now. Basically a guy would come in and say, "I need a hundred bucks." He'd fill out an application and he'd say he'd worked for the railroad for twelve years and makes this sort of money and doesn't have any debts and he's got two kids; and the bank says, "Yeah, we'll loan you one hundred dollars. Your payments, including interest, will be eight dollars and eighty-three cents a month for twelve months."

Or the Toggery, a men's clothing store, comes in and says, "I want to buy a bunch of suits and I need three thousand bucks."

The bank says, "Fine. How long?"

"Ninety days."

"Sign here. The interest is 6 percent."

Back then the lending business was mostly just small loans to individual persons and small businesses. You didn't have the huge businesses that are out there now. It was the Toggery and Gazin's and the Crystal Saloon and . . . .

When I started making loans at the Bank of Nevada in the 1950s there was no such thing as a five-year amortized business loan. That was too risky. You did make some real estate loans, but in the old days there was a rule of thumb that if you had over 40 percent of your liabilities in real estate loans, you were getting too high. That's what started the savings and loan industry. (As a rule, back then if you got over 60 percent of your total liabilities in *any* kind of loans, you were high. Hell, I know guys now who're running over 100 percent loaned out. They don't have enough liabilities to cover it. They are borrowing to do this.)

In Las Vegas a guy named Harry Gray took up some of the slack in real estate loans: he made a lot of loans to people who wanted to buy houses but couldn't get money from a bank. He and a guy named Swannee Peterson were willing to take the risk. Ten years was a long loan in those days, but they'd make you a loan on a house and take the house as security, whereas a bank didn't want it. That sort of thing wasn't a bit uncommon back then.

A lot of loans that the bank was making were character loans, which required pretty good personal knowledge of the community and of most of its citizens. A guy might come up to me on the street in Vegas in the 1950s and say, "Hey, Art, I need forty thousand bucks."

I'd say, "I ain't going to be in this afternoon, but you go see so-and-so and I'll call him." Not a lot of that goes on anymore. [laughter]

You knew everybody in those days. In today's environment someone comes in for a loan, and the first thing the bank says is, "You need one hundred thousand dollars for what? Show me! Let me see your balance sheet. Let me see your last year's tax return."

The guy says, "What do you want that for?"

"Because I want to find out if you're telling the truth about what you made last year. If you're telling me you made a hundred thousand, but you told Uncle Sam you made fifty, you're lying to one of us." [laughter]

Back then you wouldn't do that. You'd count on the manager or the lending officer, whoever he was, to know your customers. We didn't even have lines of credit in those days. If you wanted to borrow something, you'd just come in and sign your note.

# Index

Latter Day Saints, Church of Jesus Christ of, 3, 4, 10-11, 30, 108-109
Laxalt, Paul D., 119-120
Leigon, Ralph, 112
Licensing, Gaming (New Jersey), 153
Lockridge, Jay G., Jr., 205
Loetterle, Vern, 175-178

## M

McDonald, Herb, 104
Madison, Mattie, 82
Manchester Savings Bank, 83, 84
Mantle, Evelyn, 8
Mapes Hotel, 164, 166
Martinelli, Ernest, 135-136, 157, 177, 181, 185-187, 195
Masons, 108-109
Master Card International, 159
Master Charge Card, 156-159
Meany, George, 116
Middle Fork Lodge, 144-145
Mormons, Mormonism, Mormon Church. *See* Latter Day Saints, Church of Jesus Christ of

Mudge, Roland, 135
Myers, Jess, 101

## N

Navy Air Corps, 40-60, 67-68
Nevada Nuclear Test Site, 112-114
*Nevada State Journal*, 23

## O

Ogle, William, 112
Olathe, Kansas, 50-51

## P

Park, John S., 85
Patriarch, Raymond, 120
Pecetti, Tony, 69
Peterson, Cliff, 160
Peterson, Swannee, 210
Petty, Richard, 187
Pinola, Joseph, 186, 187-188, 189-190, 195
Pioneer Club, 65-66
Pony Express Motel, 167
Possum, Polly, 174
Prather, Gaylord K., 180-183

Prell, Milton, 116
Pyramid Lake, 58-60

Q

Questa, Edward J., 86, 91,
129, 181

R

Recordak, 204
Reno, 127-130, 132, 137,
139, 143, 147, 160-169
*Reno Evening Gazette*, 23
Reno High School, 28-29
Risso, Al, 135
Riverside Hotel, 164, 166
Robert H. Mitchell Elementary School, 7-8
Roman Catholic Church,
107-109
Roosevelt, Franklin D.,
128

S

*Sable*, 54
St. Mary's College, 47-50
Sample, Alex K., Jr., 179-
180
San Francisco, California,
12

Sawyer, Grant, 119
Sbragia, Joseph J., 39,
135, 137-138, 205
Security Bank, 186
Sheppard, Maurice, 147
Siart, William E. B., 186-
191
Siegel, Benjamin "Bugsy,"
90-91
Smith (née Mathews),
Annie, 13-14
Smith, Arthur M. (senior),
3-7, 9-10, 12-13, 21-22,
30
Smith, Arthur M. III, 102
Smith, Barbara, 102
Smith, Blake, 102
Smith (née Campbell),
Charlotte, 68, 99, 100-
102, 104-105, 108, 132,
199-200
Smith, Deborah K., 102
Smith (née Knudson),
Elva Evelyn, 3, 5, 8-9,
21-22, 193
Smith, Joseph A., 13-14
Smith, Margery, 8
Smith, Ralph, 21
Smith, Raymond I.
"Pappy," 143, 163
Southern Nevada Industrial Foundation (SNIF),
89, 91
Southern Pacific Railroad,
3, 42, 203-204

# Photo Credits